FIRST-WORLD CAT PROBLEMS

What am I doing with my lives?

POP PRESS

1 3 5 7 9 10 8 6 4 2

Pop Press, an imprint of Ebury Publishing,
20 Vauxhall Bridge Road,
London, SW1V 2SA

Pop Press is part of the Penguin Random House group of companies whose
addresses can be found at global.penguinrandomhouse.com

Copyright © Pop Press 2018
Captions by Pesala Bandara
Photo research by Michelle Warner

First published by Pop Press in 2018

www.penguin.co.uk

A CIP catalogue record for this book is available from the British Library

ISBN 9781785039621

Printed and bound in China by Toppan Leefung

Penguin Random House is committed to a sustainable future for
our business, our readers and our planet. This book is made from
Forest Stewardship Council® certified paper.

I'll never look as good as the cats in the Whiskers commercials.

I caught my owner looking at other cats on the internet.

But I had salmon for breakfast too.

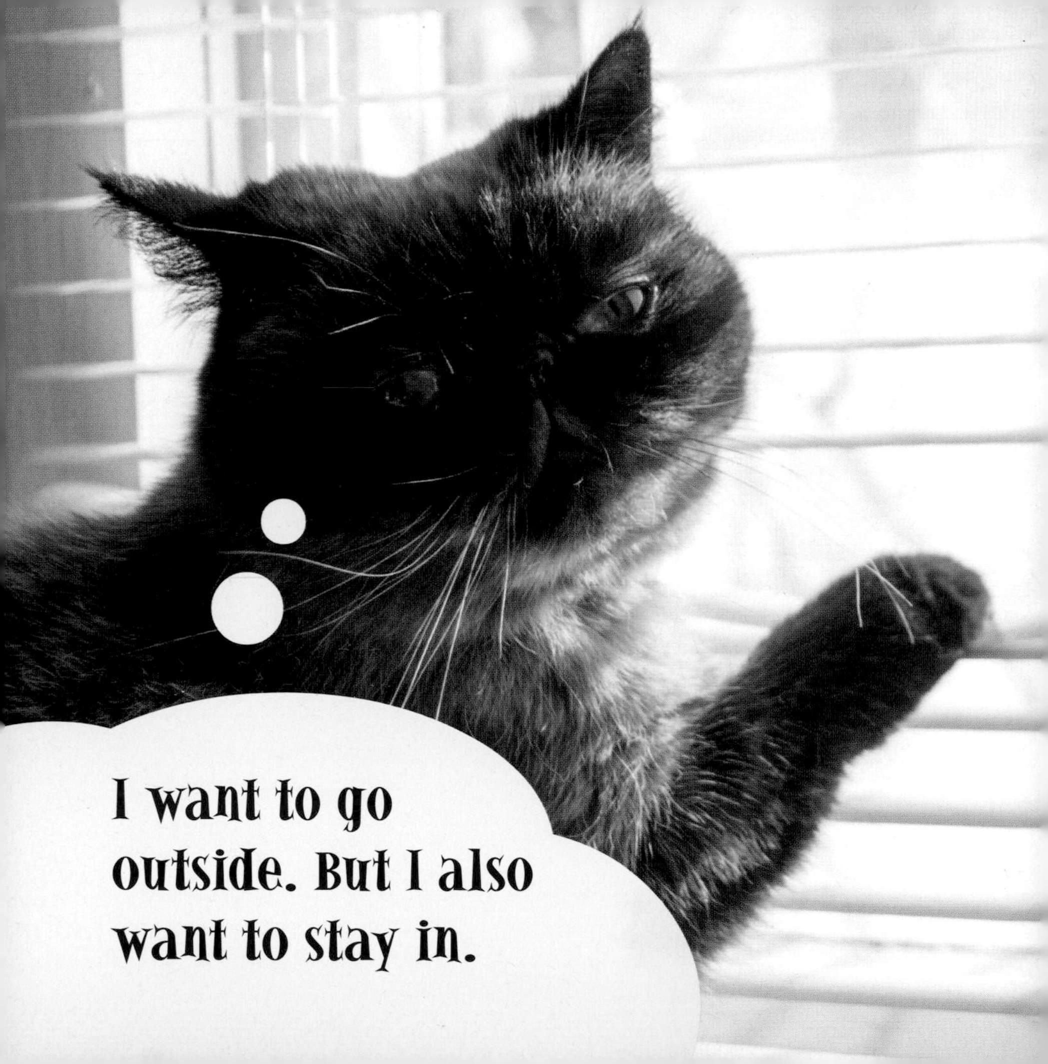
I want to go outside. But I also want to stay in.

I only got 14 hours of sleep today.

I tried to jump
out of the window,
but landed on my feet.

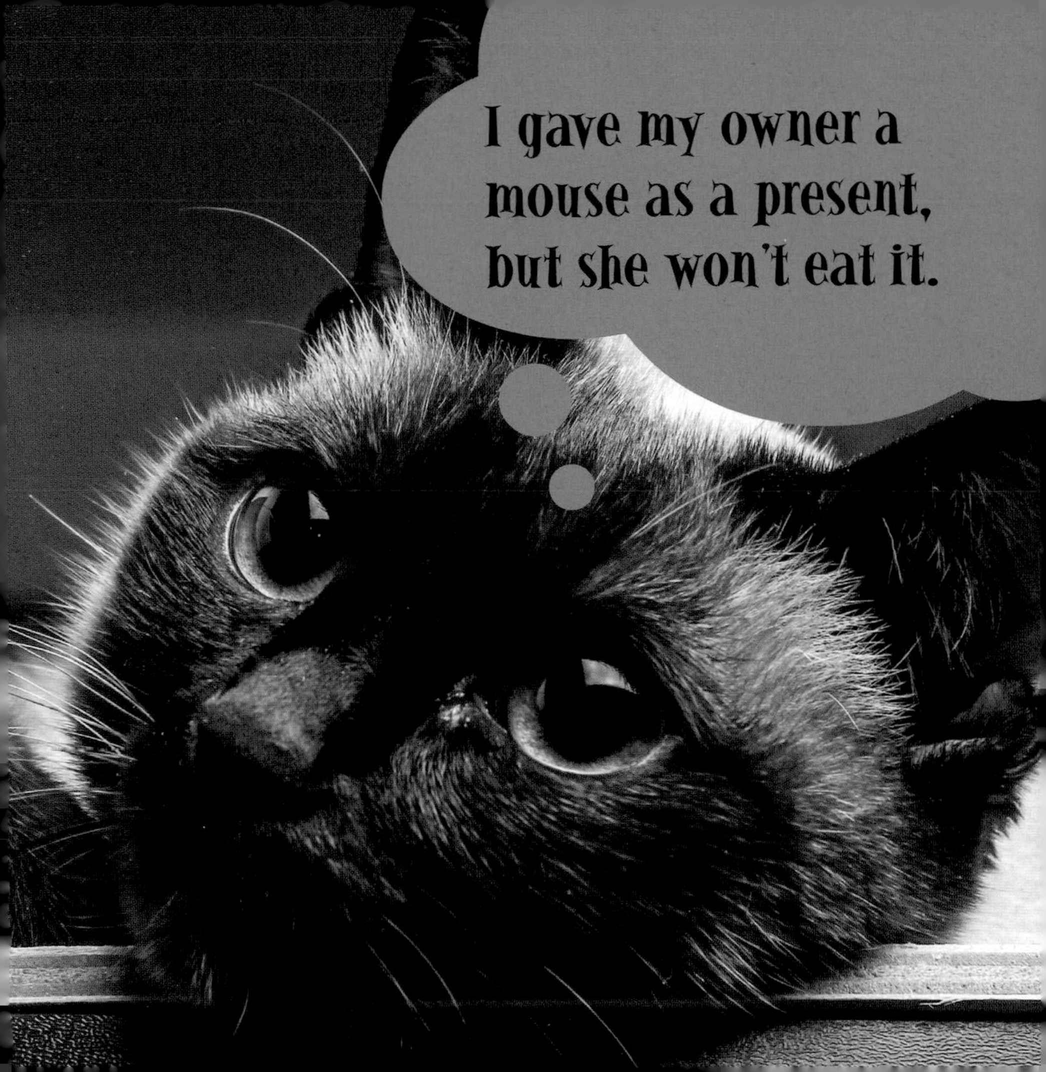
I gave my owner a mouse as a present, but she won't eat it.

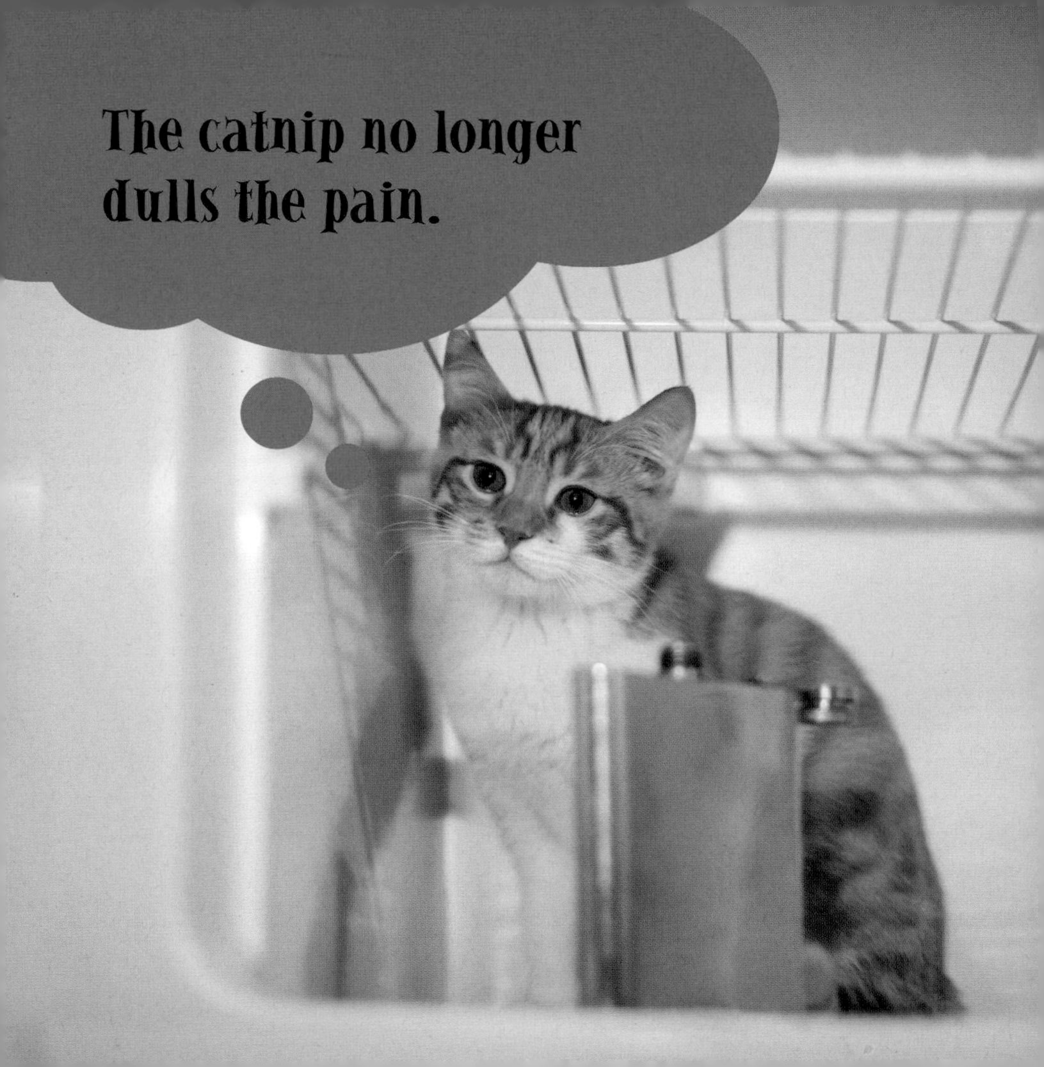
The catnip no longer dulls the pain.

Did I ask you to touch my tail?

She has two hands, but only uses one of them to pet me.

I haven't eaten all day (not counting breakfast because I threw it up on the rug).

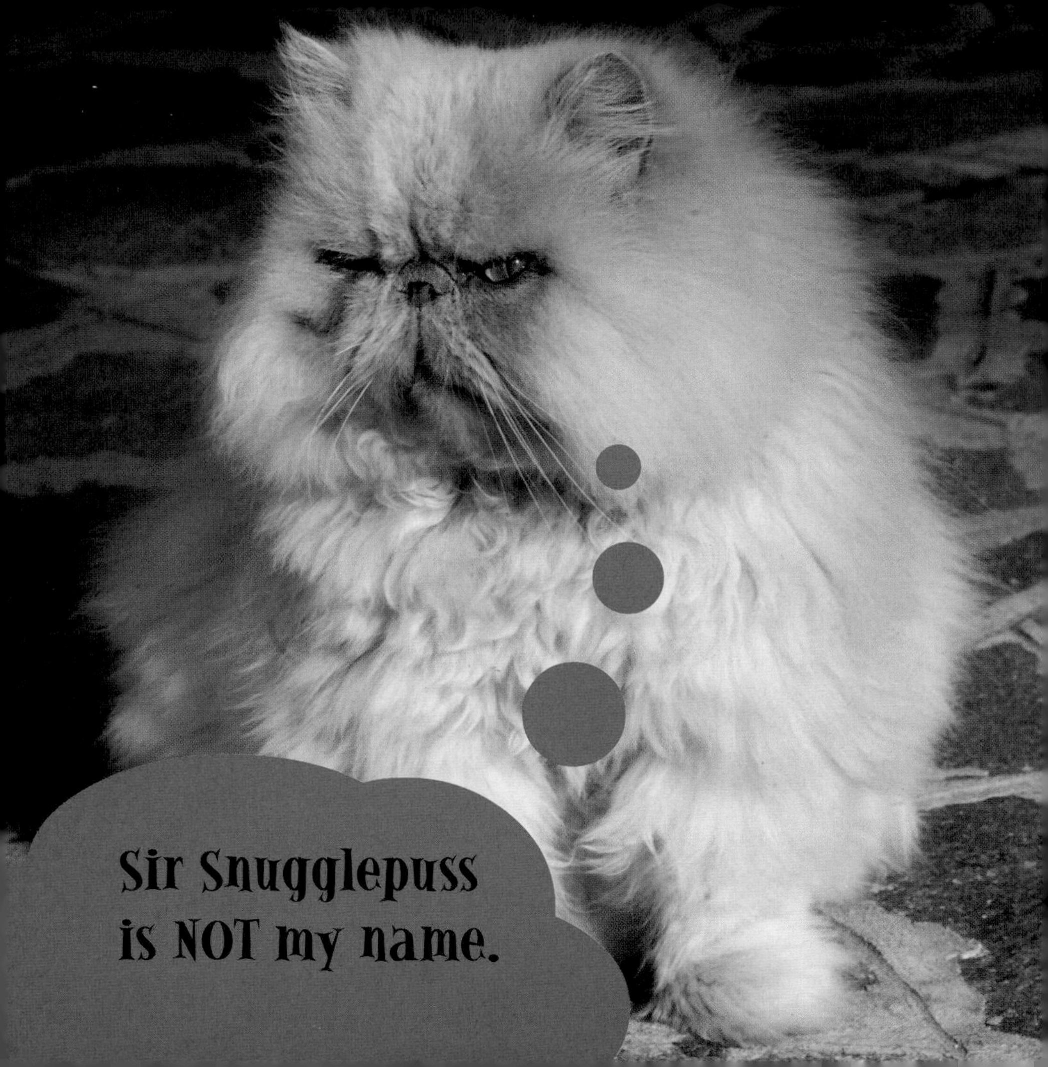
Sir Snugglepuss
is NOT my name.

I can't decide whether to nap on the sofa or the sink. Why can't life be simple?

What if that bird
had a family?

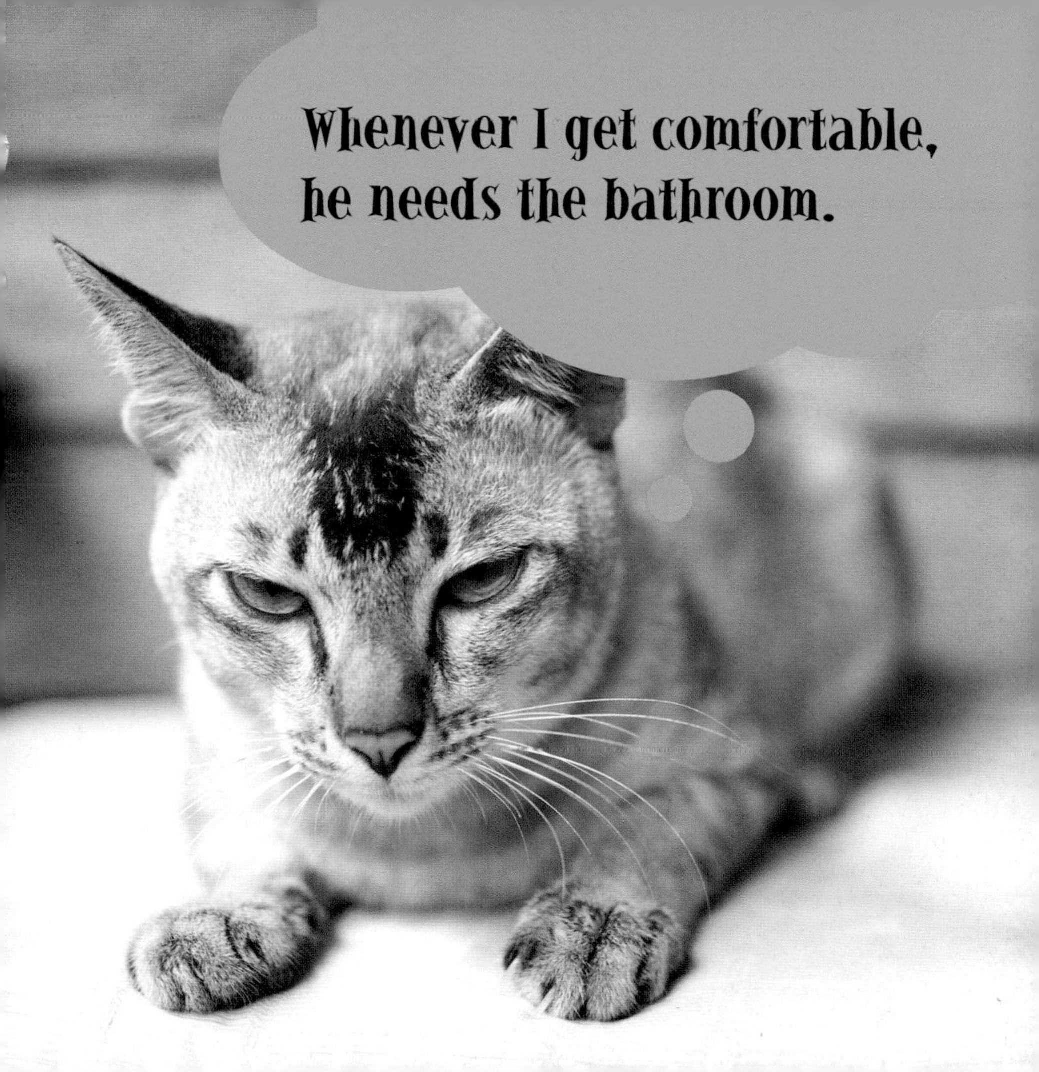
Whenever I get comfortable,
he needs the bathroom.

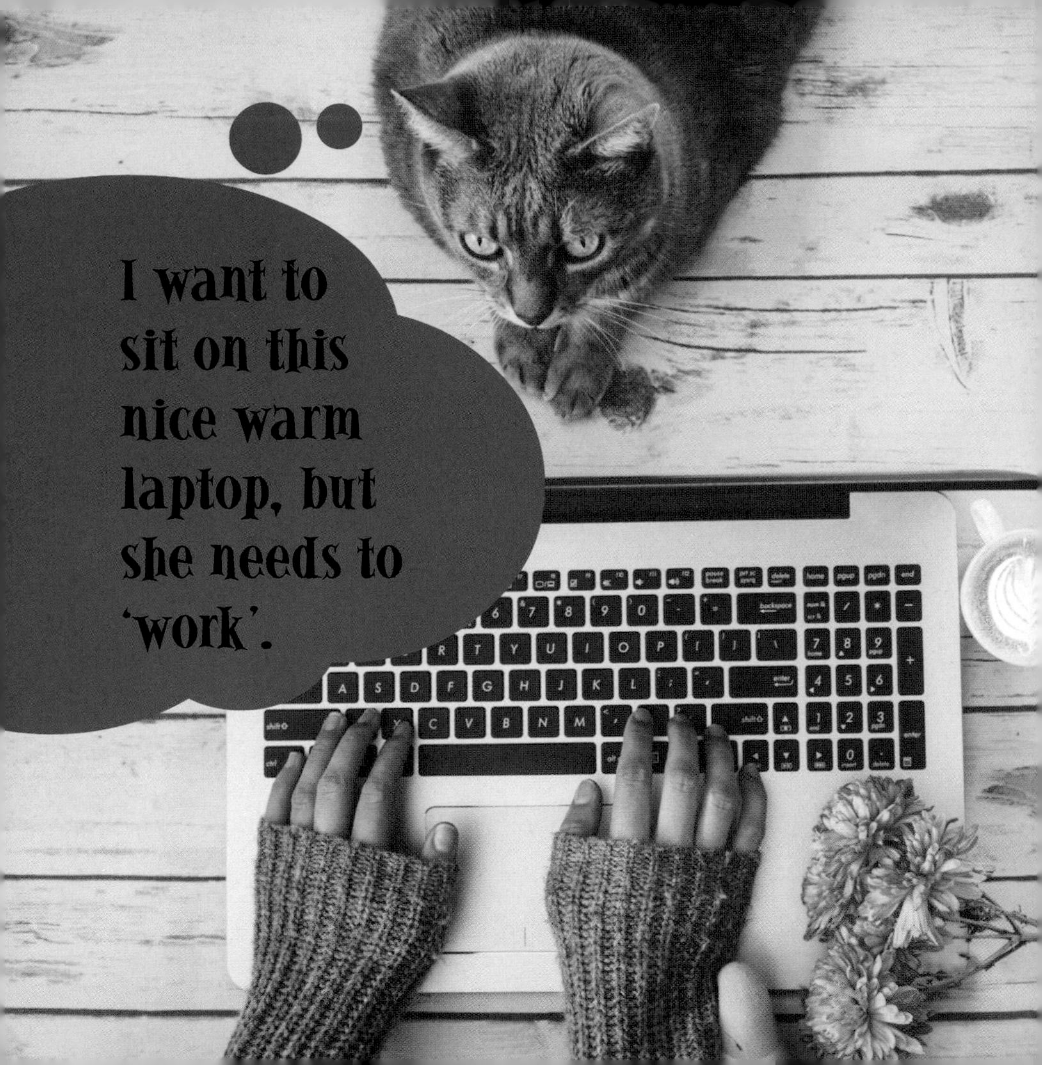
I want to sit on this nice warm laptop, but she needs to 'work'.

You have room for all these clothes, but you're leaving me behind?

She fell asleep after only stroking my left side. Now I'm all uneven.

Why don't you think I'm good enough without these ridiculous outfits?

Wake me up when you've got something interesting to say.

My owner won't hold the door open for five minutes while I decide if I actually want to come in.

I can see the bottom of my food bowl. I think they're trying to starve me.

I'm too tired to get the treat my owner dropped on the other side of the room.

My favourite toy is trapped under the sofa, and I only have 64 others to choose from.

I can't believe I have to claw them every time I want to be petted. It's exhausting.

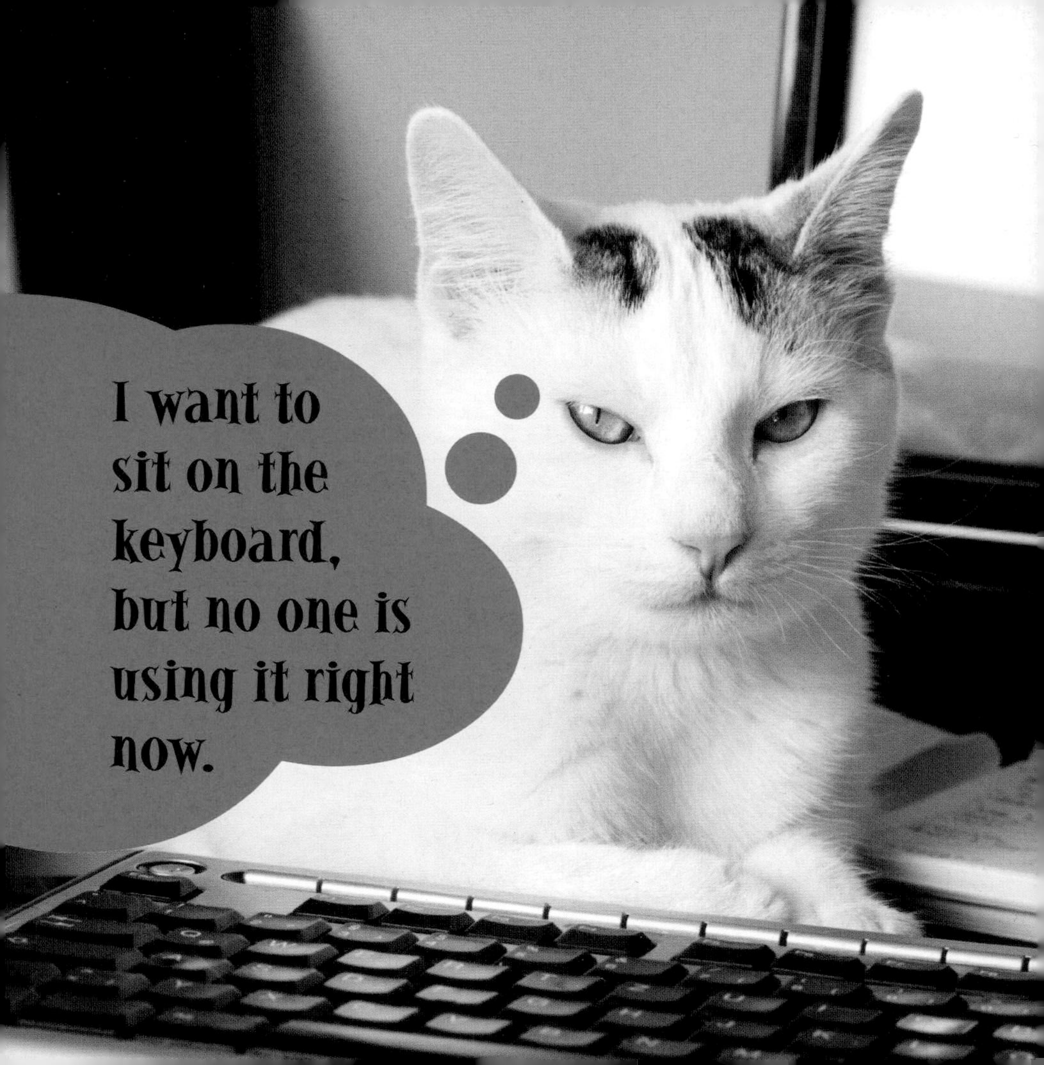
I want to sit on the keyboard, but no one is using it right now.

They used Sellotape to get all my fur off their bed. A whole day's work wasted.

I want to go outside, but I don't want to get my fur wet.

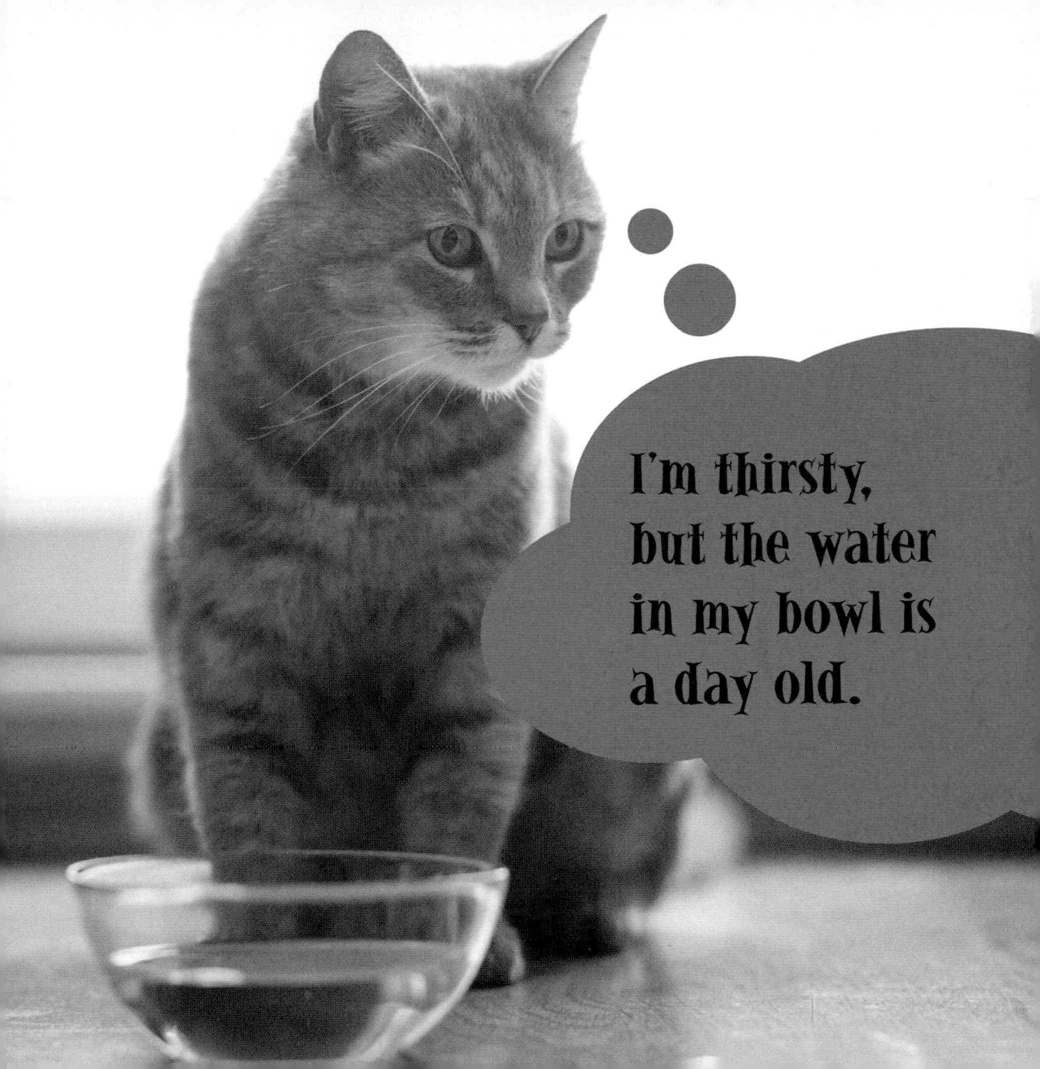
I'm thirsty, but the water in my bowl is a day old.

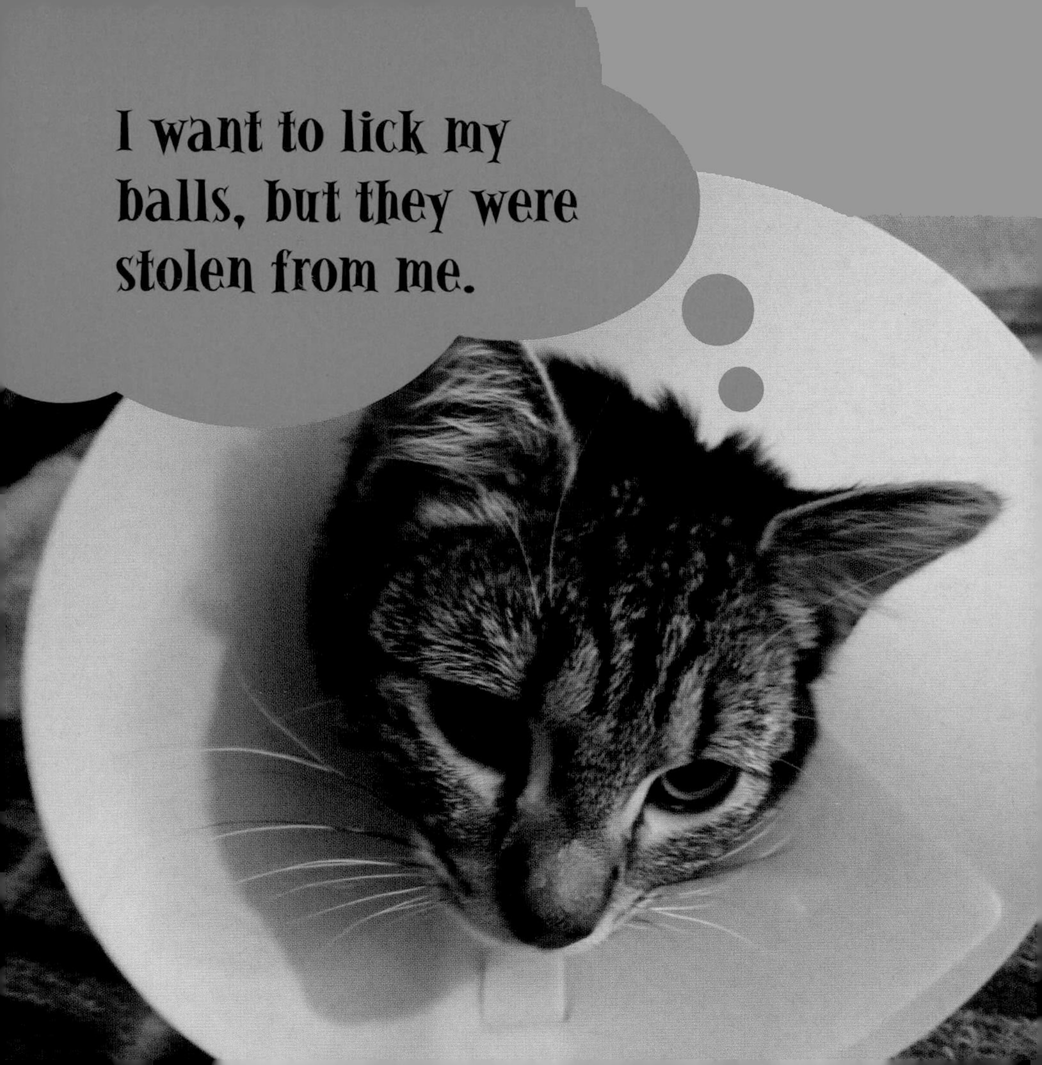
I want to lick my balls, but they were stolen from me.

I just groomed myself for two hours, then they comb me the wrong way. Now I have to start all over again.

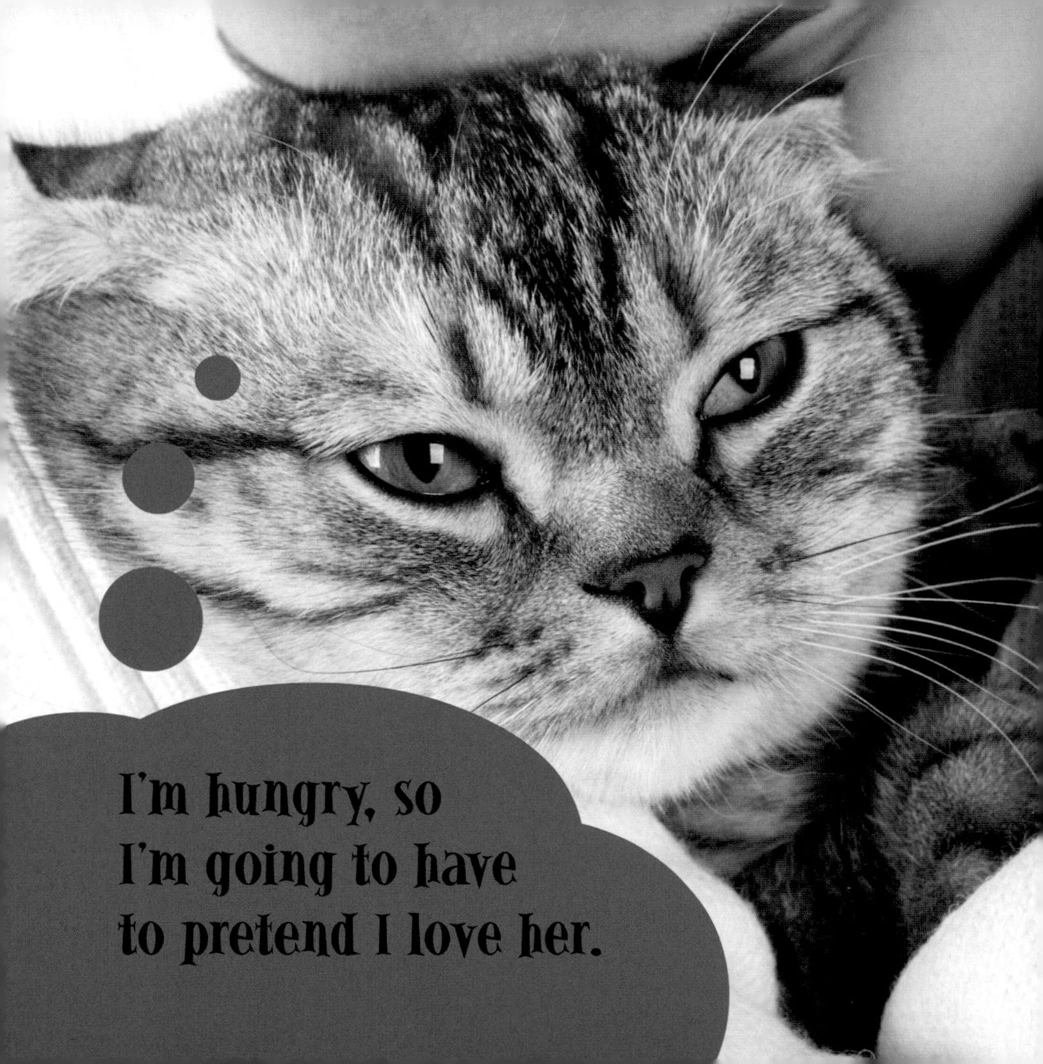
I'm hungry, so
I'm going to have
to pretend I love her.

I want to run around and make lots of noise for no reason, but it's not 2am.

They're away for the weekend and think I can live on dried food.

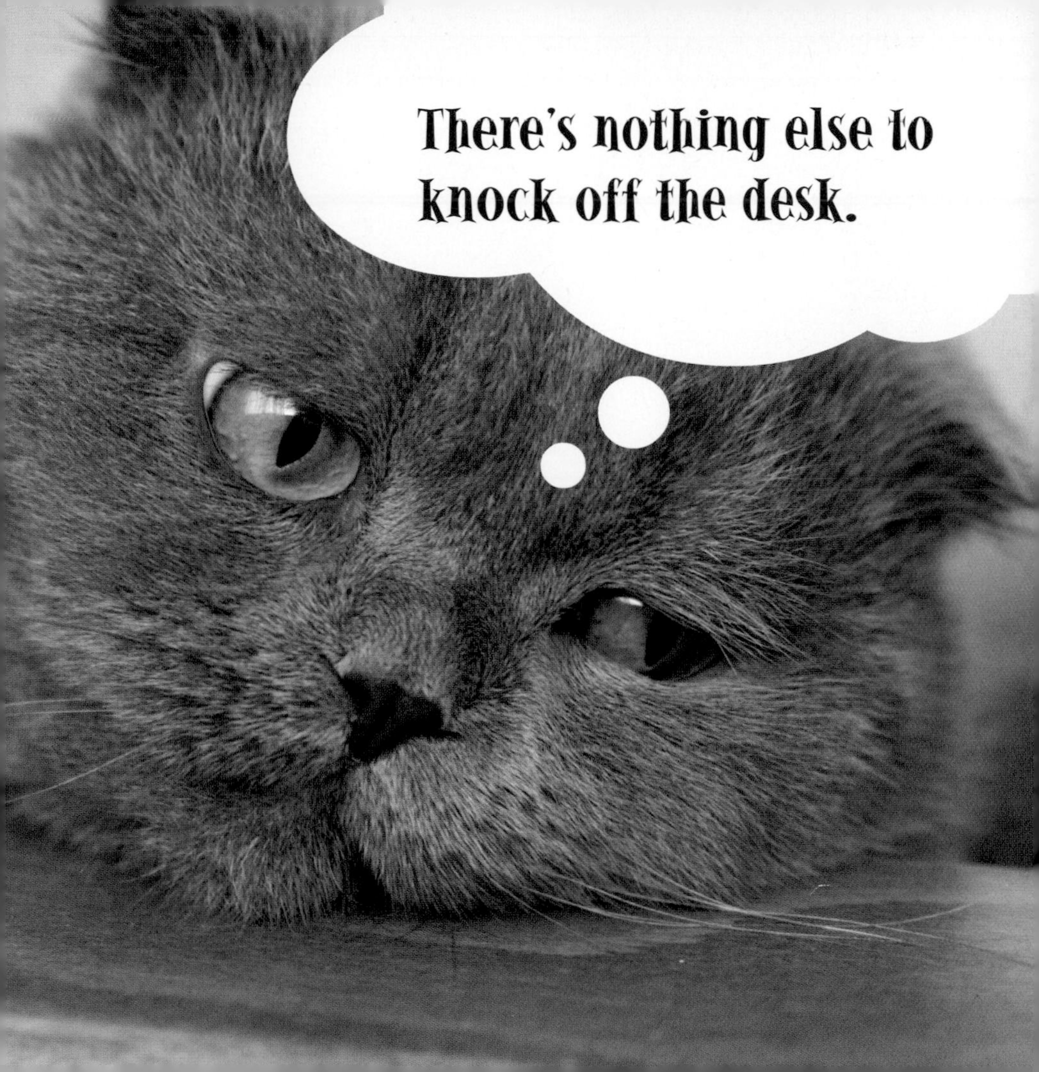
There's nothing else to knock off the desk.

I wanted my tummy tickled, but all I got was a lousy pat on the head.

They gave me a bath, even though I spent 80 per cent of the day licking myself.

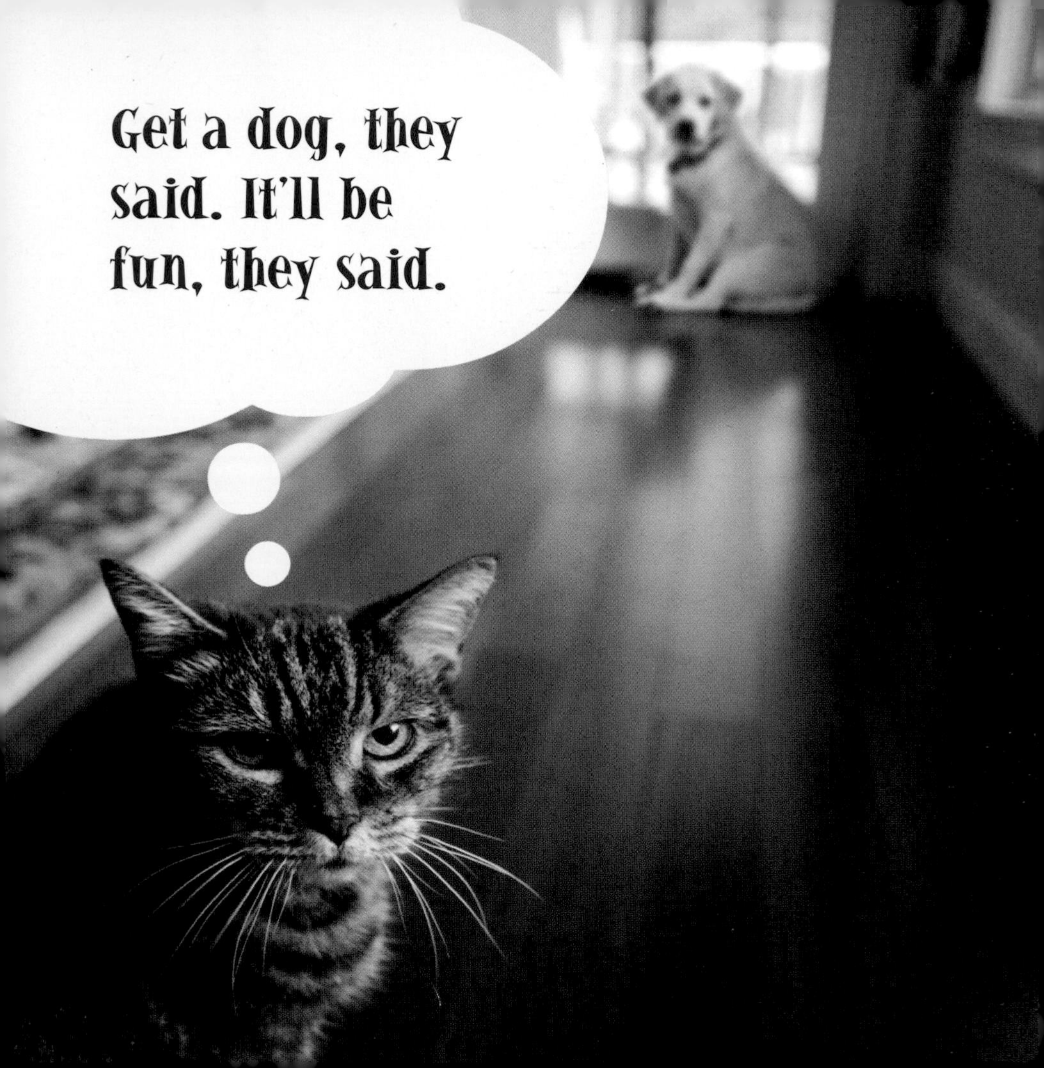
Get a dog, they said. It'll be fun, they said.

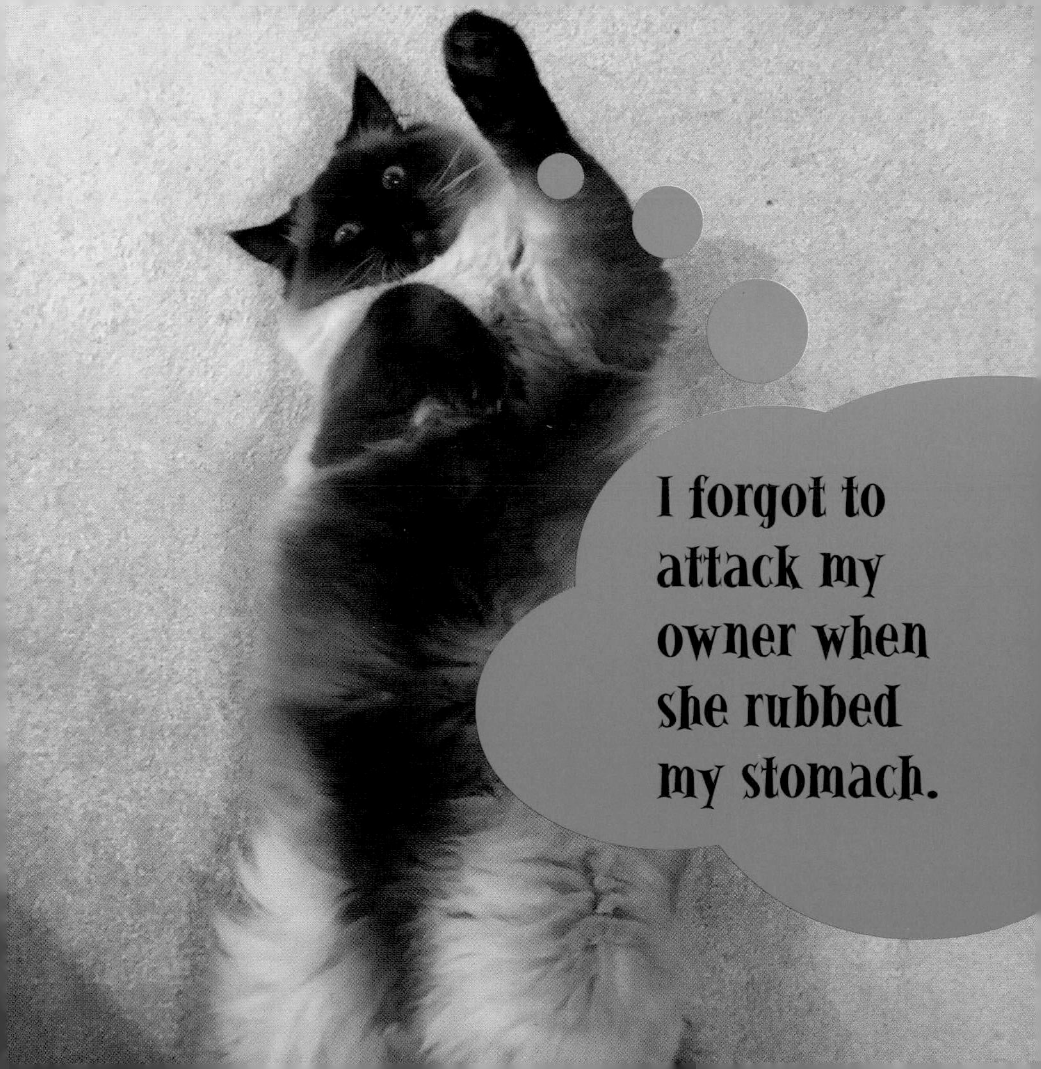
I forgot to attack my owner when she rubbed my stomach.

I missed my 1pm nap.
Now I have to wait for
my 1.15pm nap.

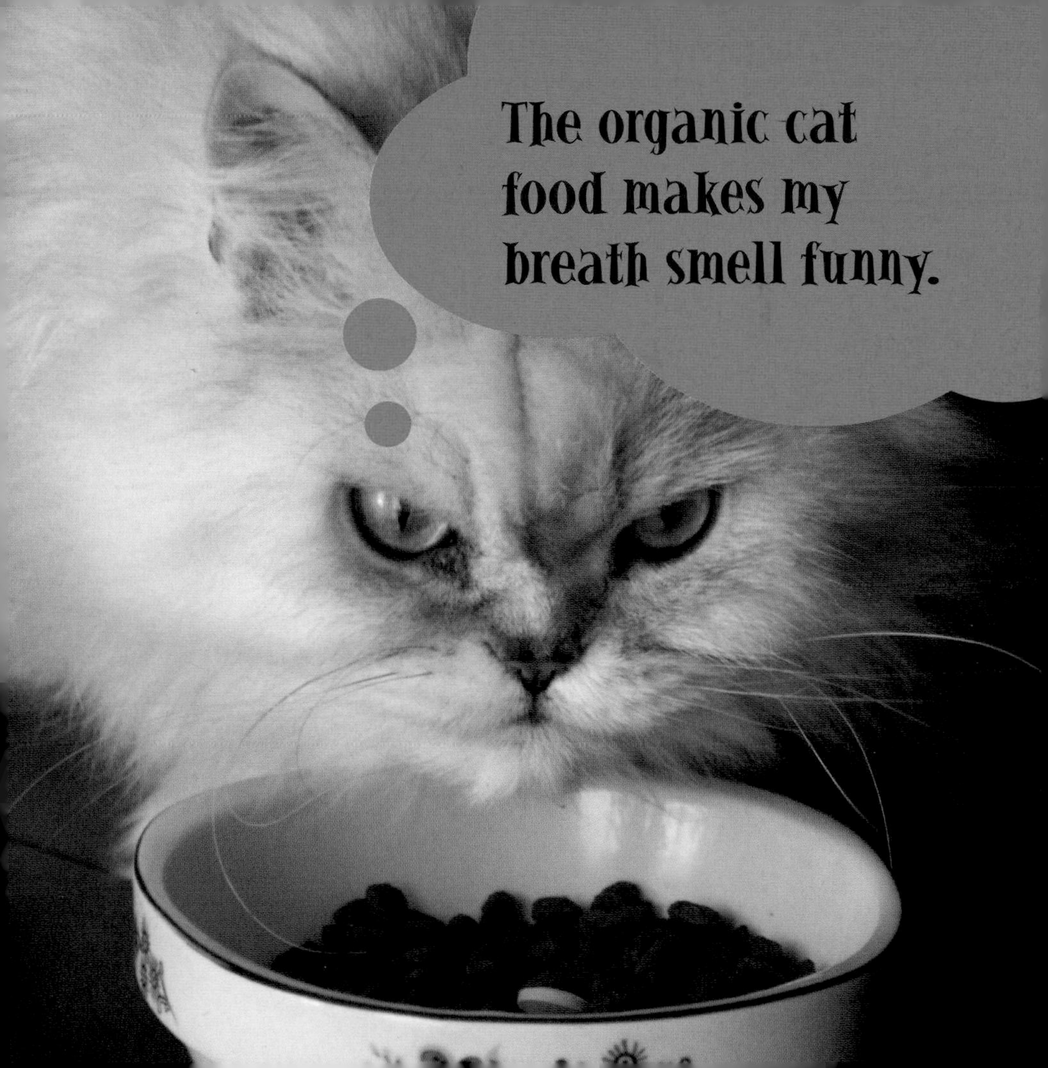
The organic cat
food makes my
breath smell funny.

I have my own Instagram page, but they won't let me veto the photos.

No matter how long I sit on her, she still prefers the book. It doesn't even purr.

No I won't spend a week in a cattery. Even one that's more expensive than the hotel you're staying in.

I was grumpy before Grumpy Cat was even born. My owners are just worse at social media.

They expect me to coexist with these fish, but never let me have a crack at them.

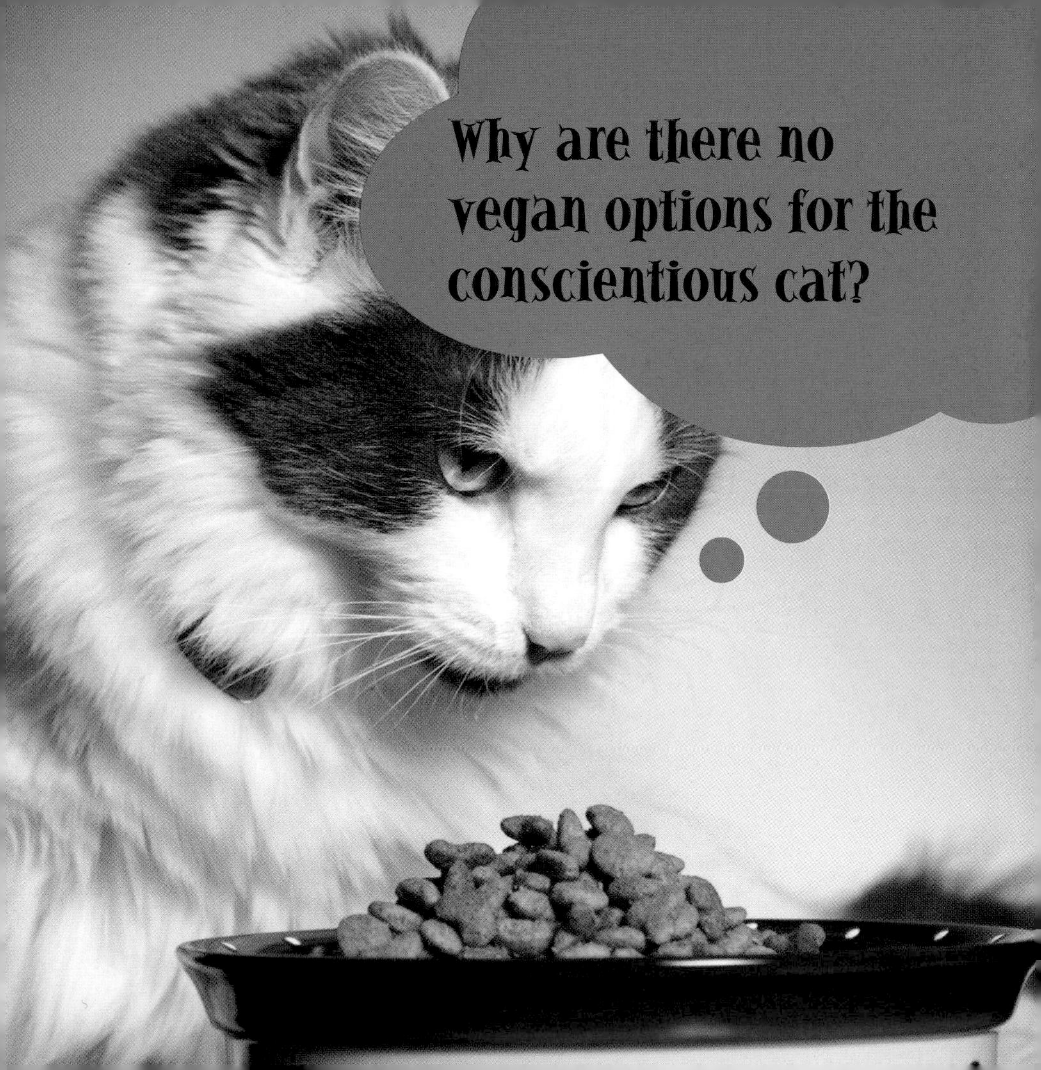
Why are there no vegan options for the conscientious cat?

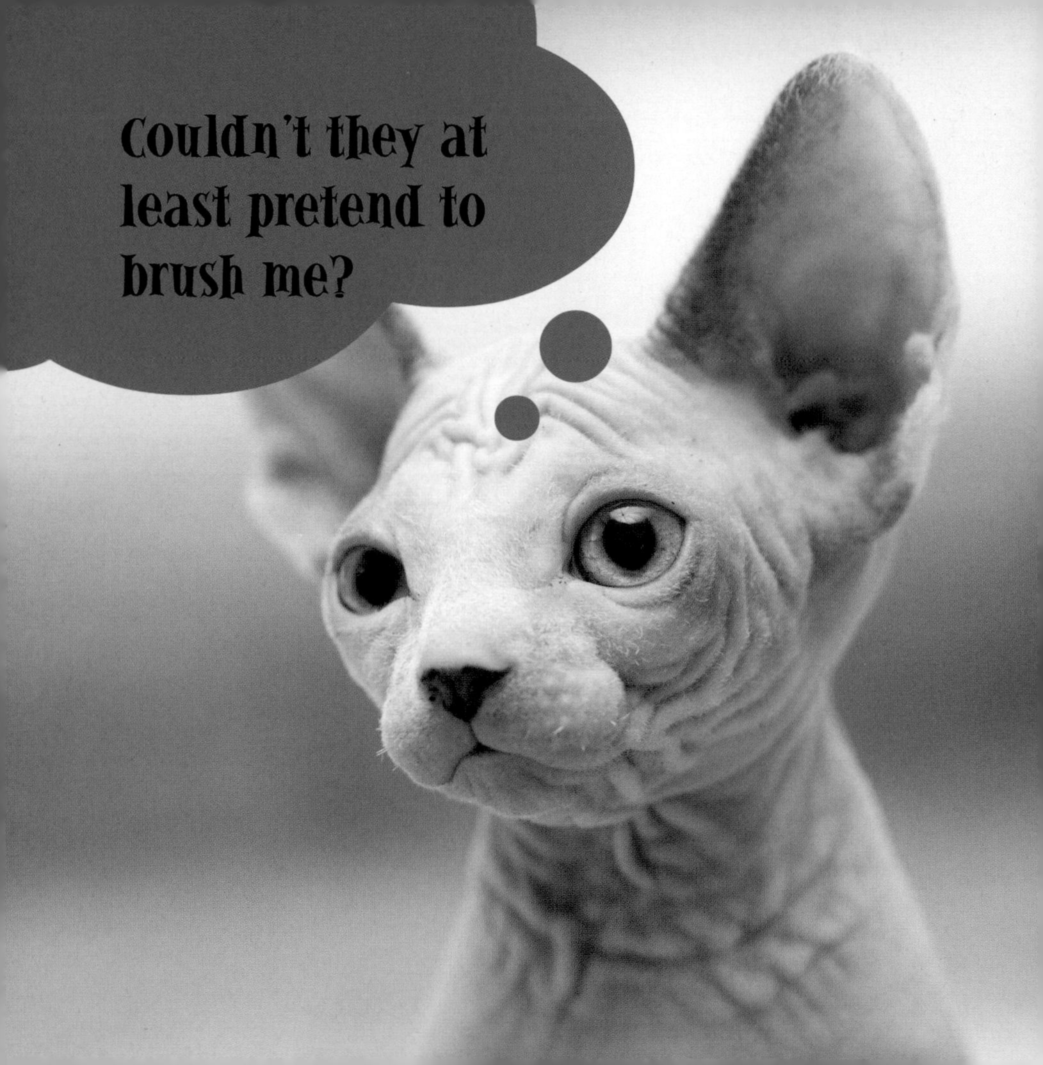
Couldn't they at least pretend to brush me?

They got a new kitten. I'm going to have to endure their strokes just so I'm not forgotten.

I try to sniff next door's bum, but she thinks she's too good for me.

Next door's cat always sniffs my bum. I'm not just a piece of meat.

They took me to a cat spa, but forgot to book my nail-buffing appointment.

I keep peeing on the kitchen floor to mark my territory, but they keep mopping it up.

The dawn chorus is supposed to be a pleasant sound, but it just reminds me of all the birds I haven't got to yet.

The red dot taunts me.

She took a photo of me sleeping, and her 72 Instagram followers saw it before I'd even woken up.

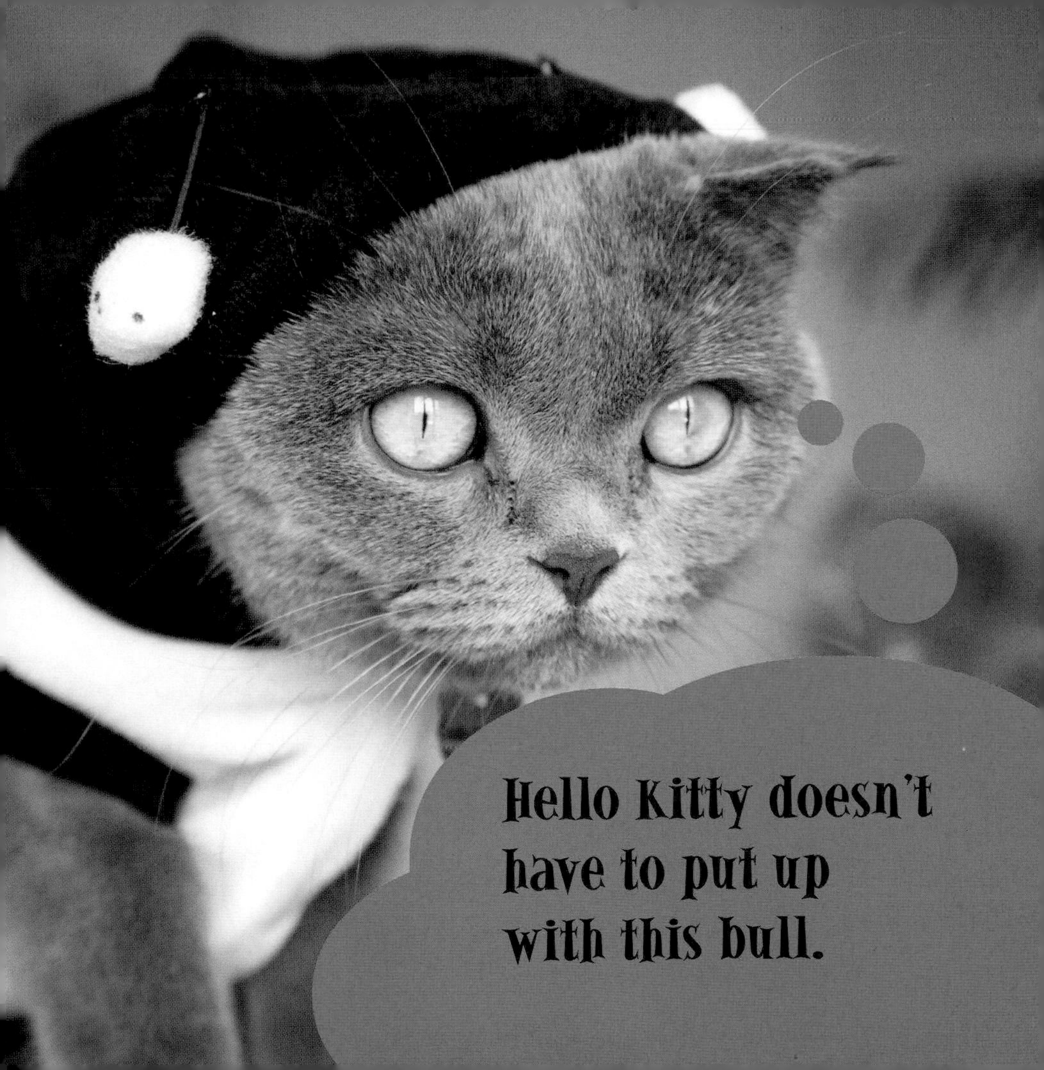
Hello Kitty doesn't have to put up with this bull.

They shut me in the spare room every time their friend with allergies comes over. That's their problem, not mine.

They try to make me sleep on this ridiculous cat bed, when the wooden chair is clearly more comfortable.

They get home at midnight and think that's ok. Don't they know I have a schedule?

I just wanted to play fight. Why do the other cats always have to make it so real?

Every time I catch it,
they take it away again.
What's the point of
anything?

I want to catch one of these fish, but I don't want to get my paw wet.

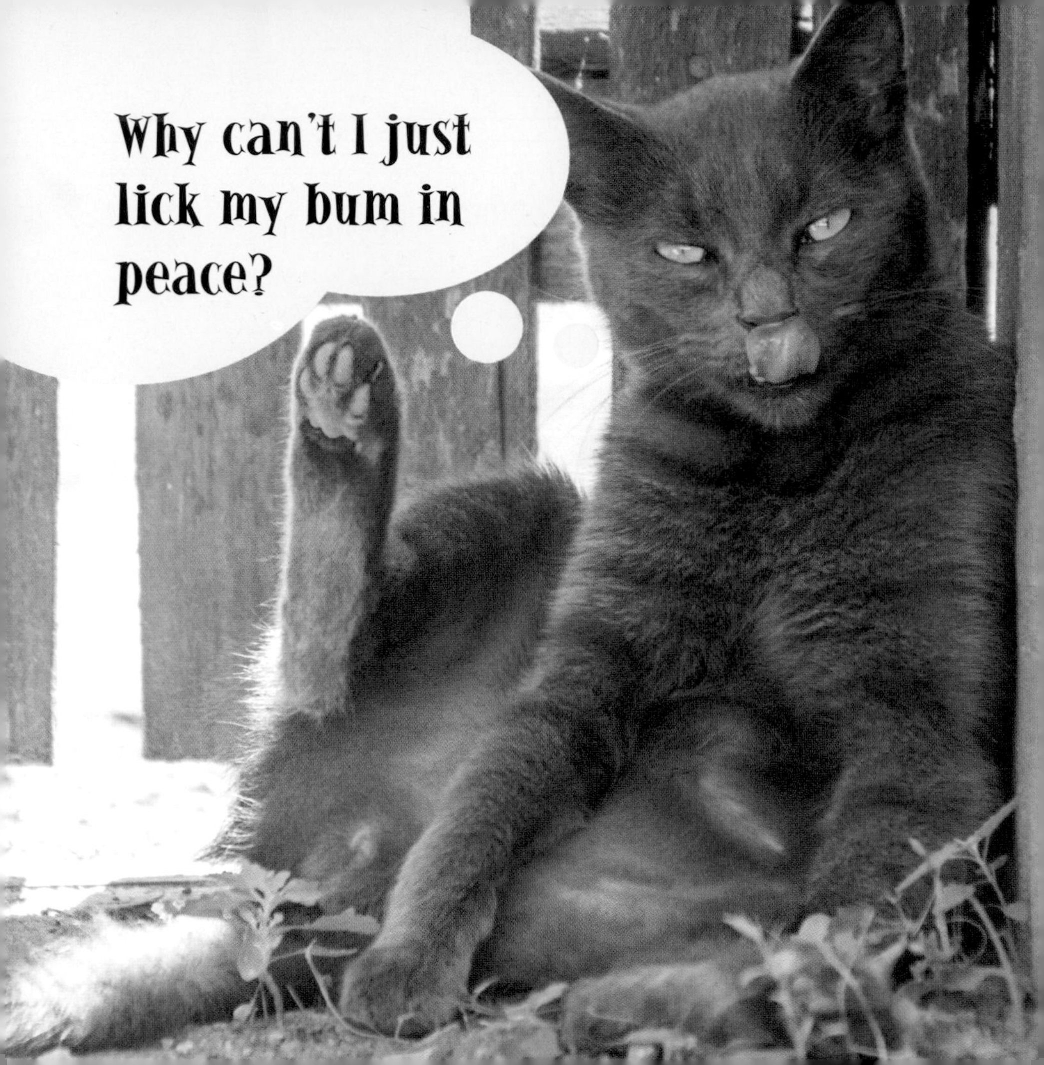
Why can't I just lick my bum in peace?

I look ridiculous.

I clearly know
how to walk myself.

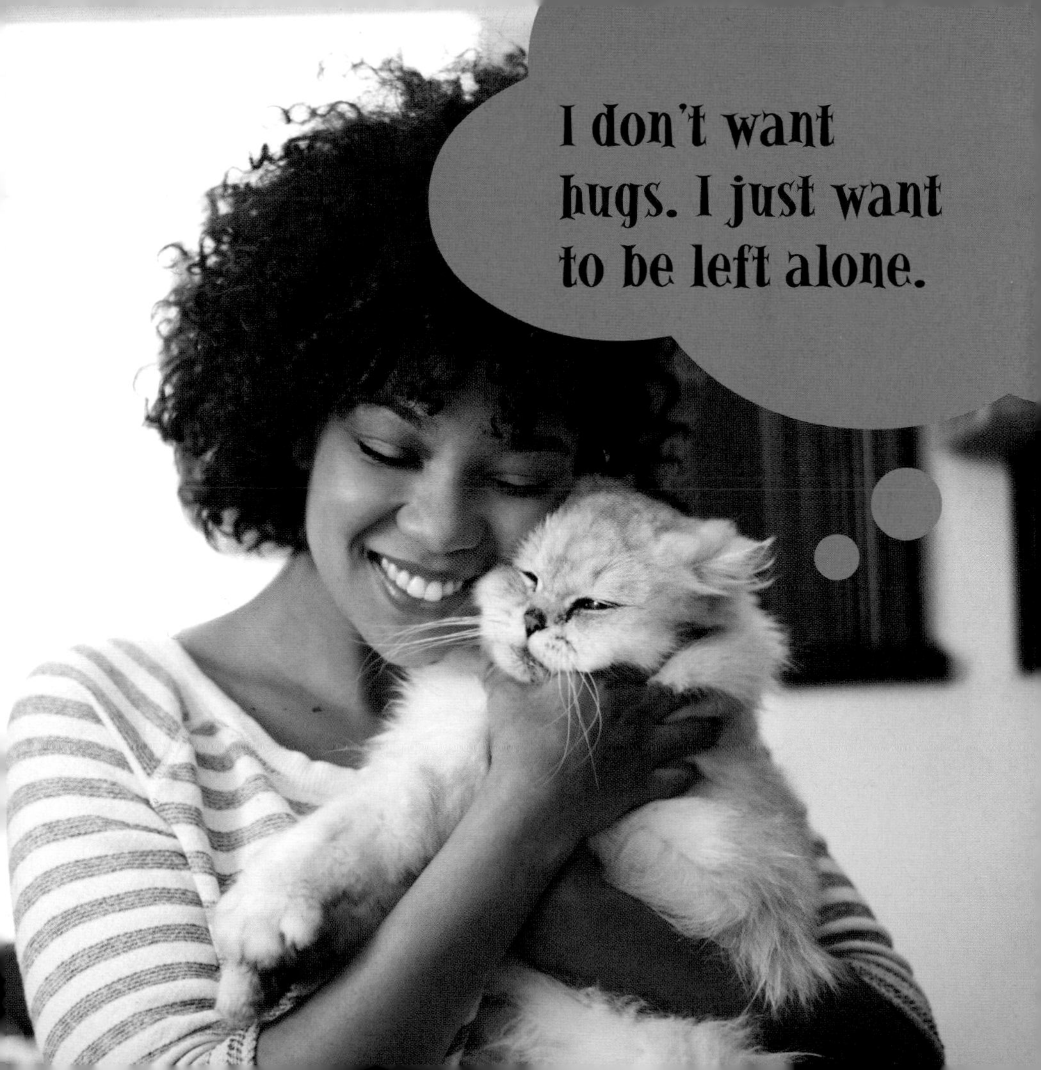
I don't want hugs. I just want to be left alone.

This patch of sunlight keeps moving.

I just want to sit on this stair without everyone tripping over me. Is that too much to ask?

I was only asleep for nine hours when that car alarm woke me up.

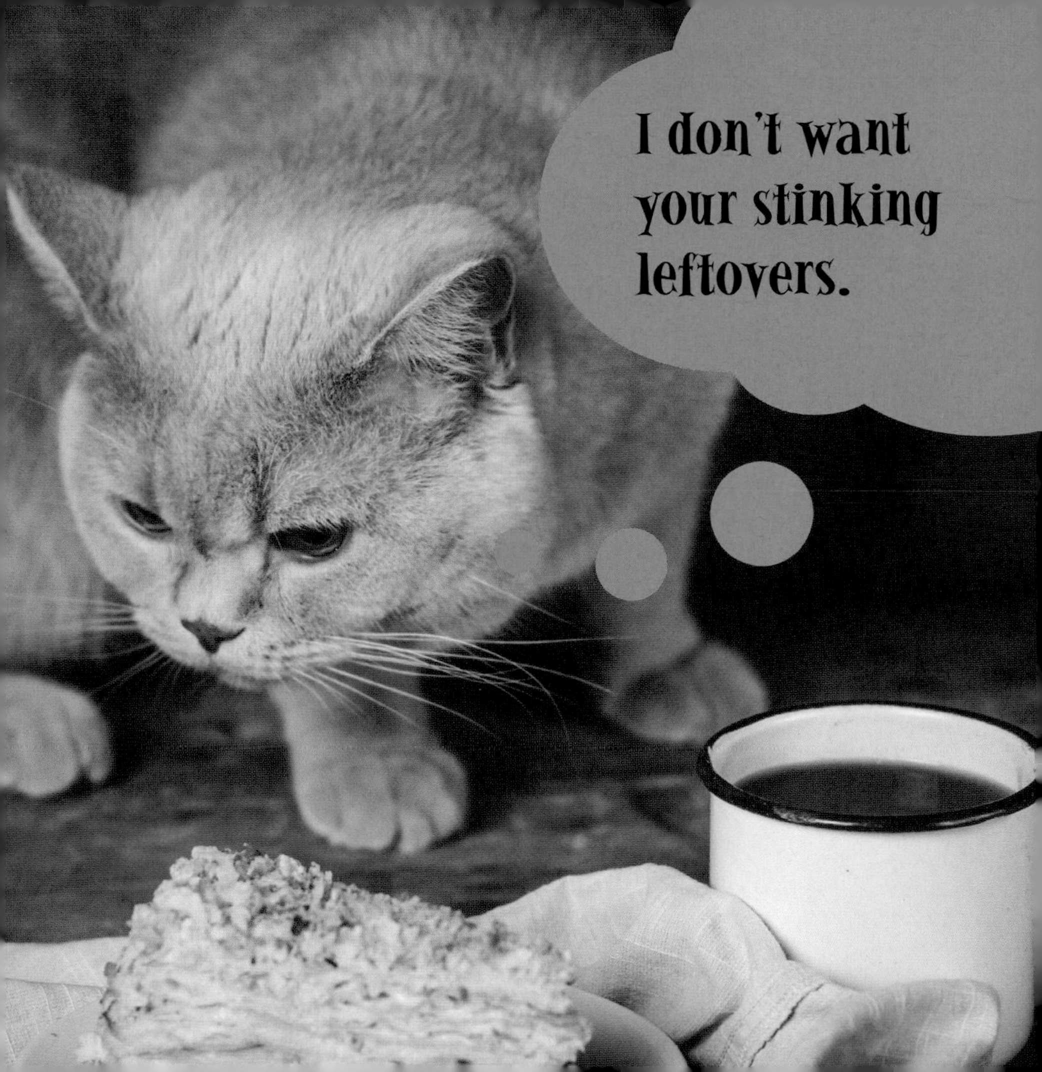
I don't want your stinking leftovers.

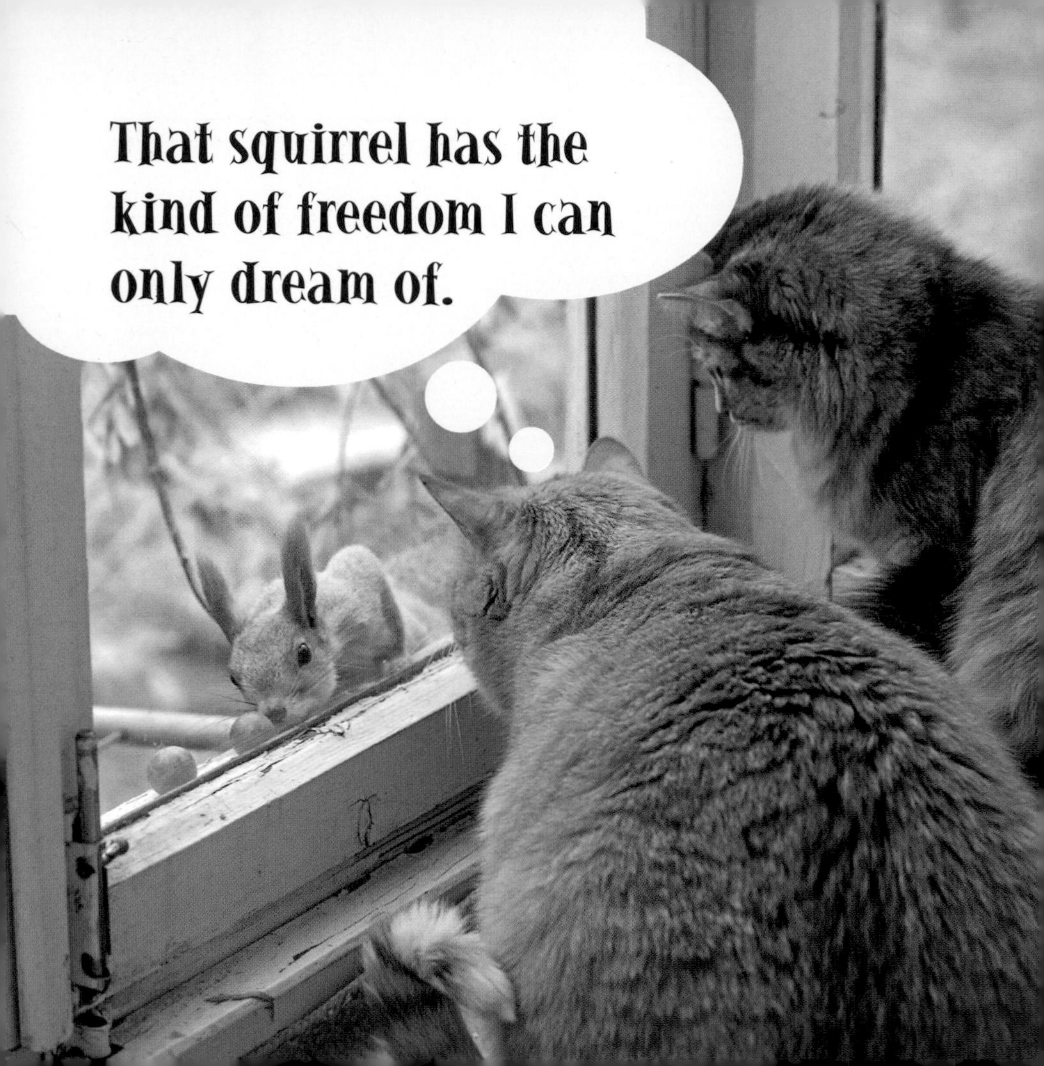
That squirrel has the kind of freedom I can only dream of.

I need my 17 hours sleep.
I've got to get up early and
unroll the toilet paper.

Ok fine, you can take one picture of me by the Christmas tree before I destroy it.

You're sitting in my favourite seat...

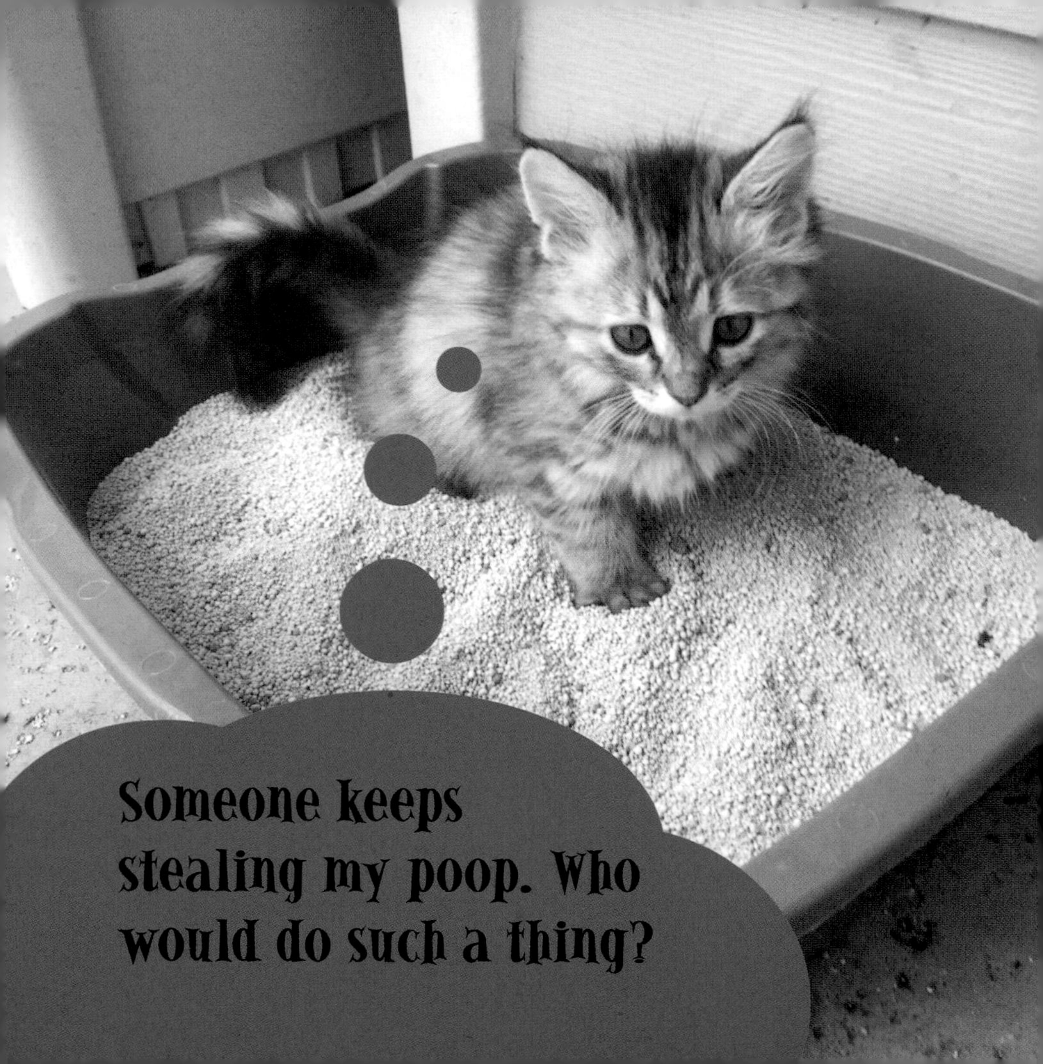
Someone keeps stealing my poop. Who would do such a thing?

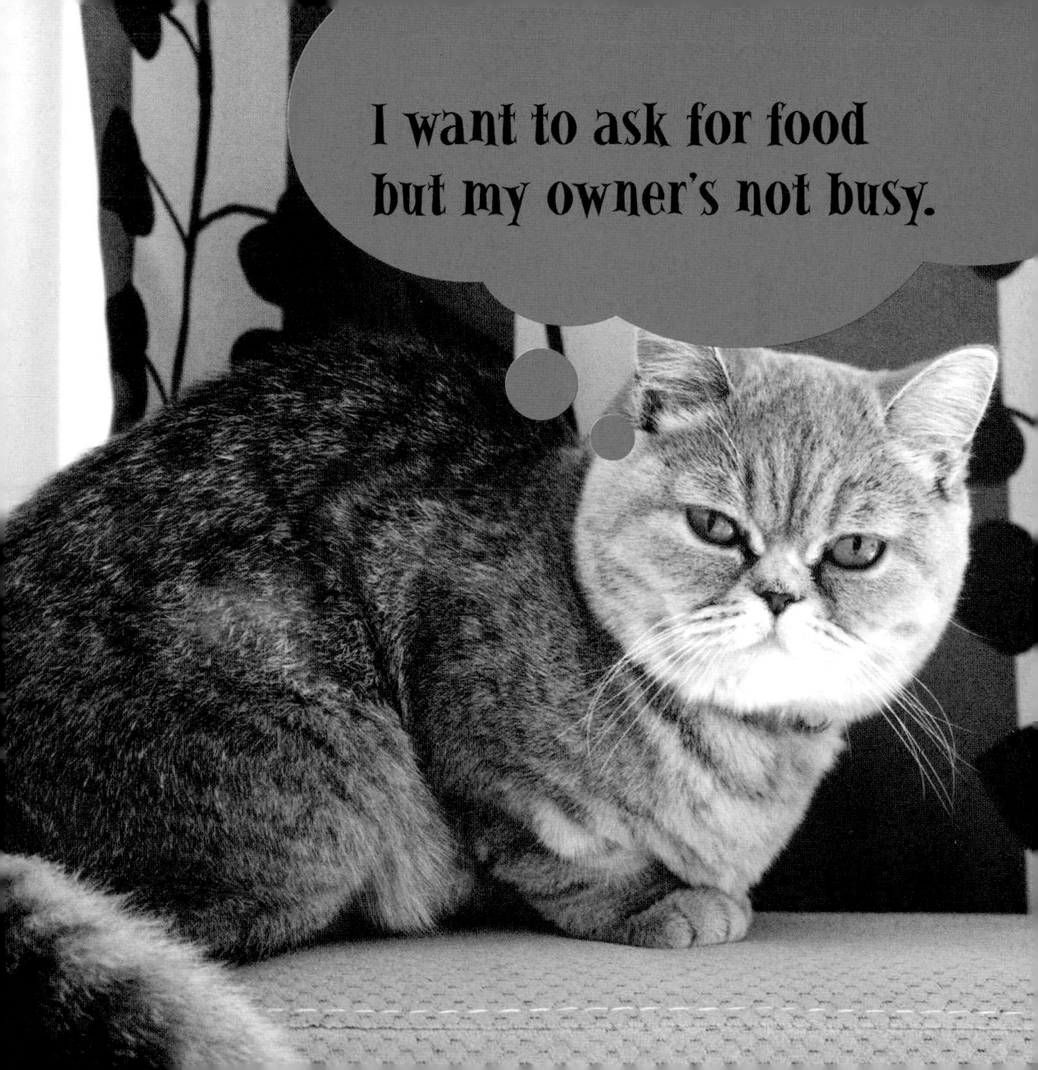
I want to ask for food
but my owner's not busy.

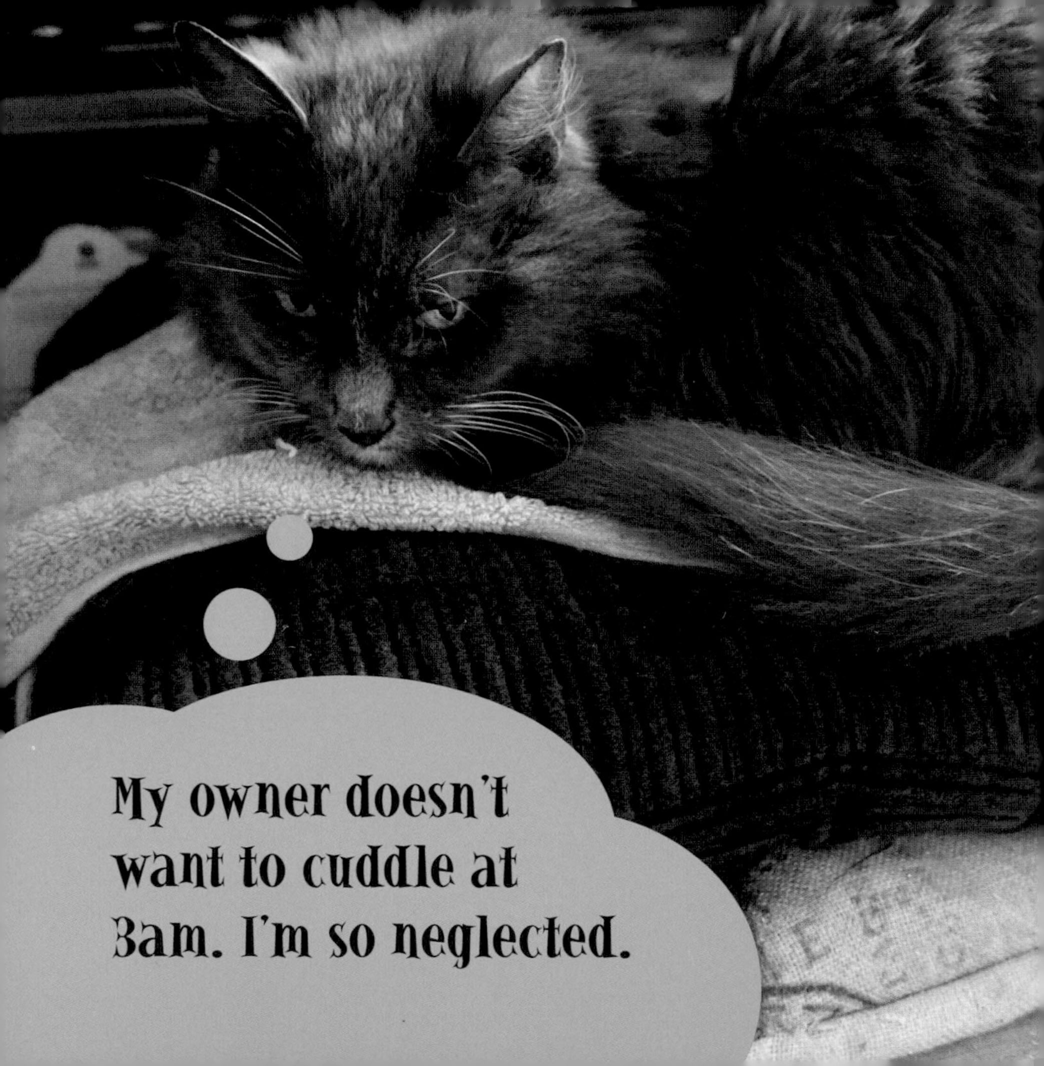
My owner doesn't want to cuddle at 3am. I'm so neglected.

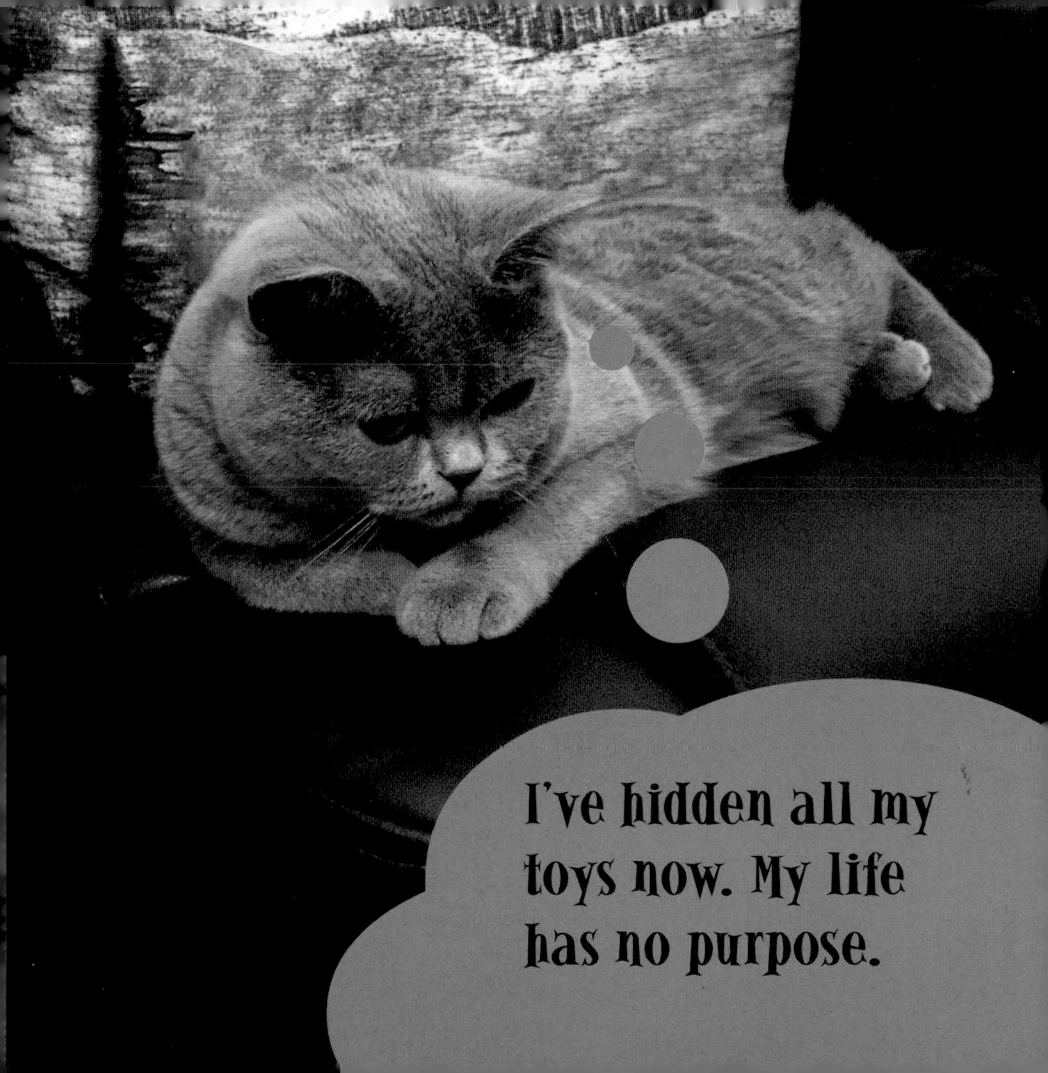
I've hidden all my toys now. My life has no purpose.

Stop breathing.
It's annoying.

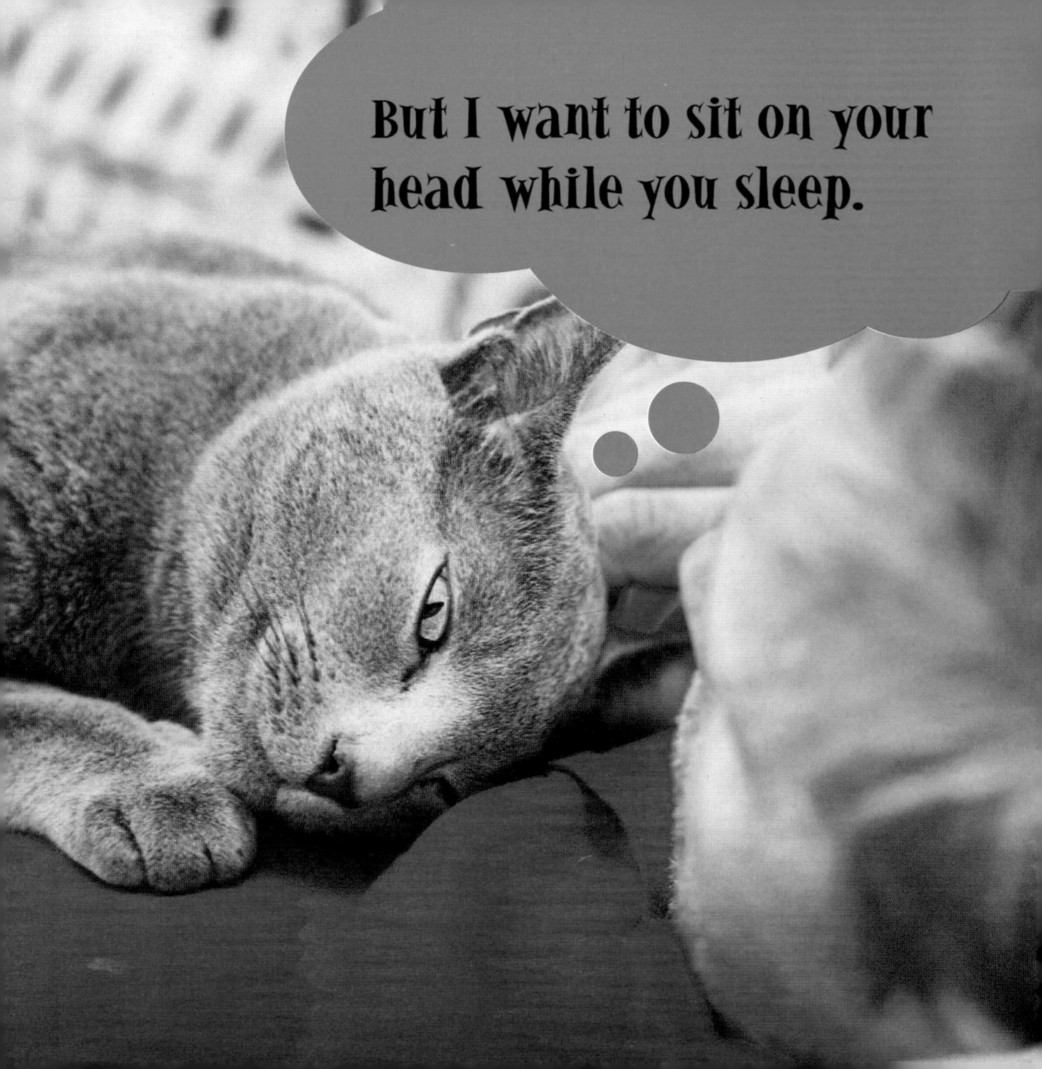
But I want to sit on your head while you sleep.

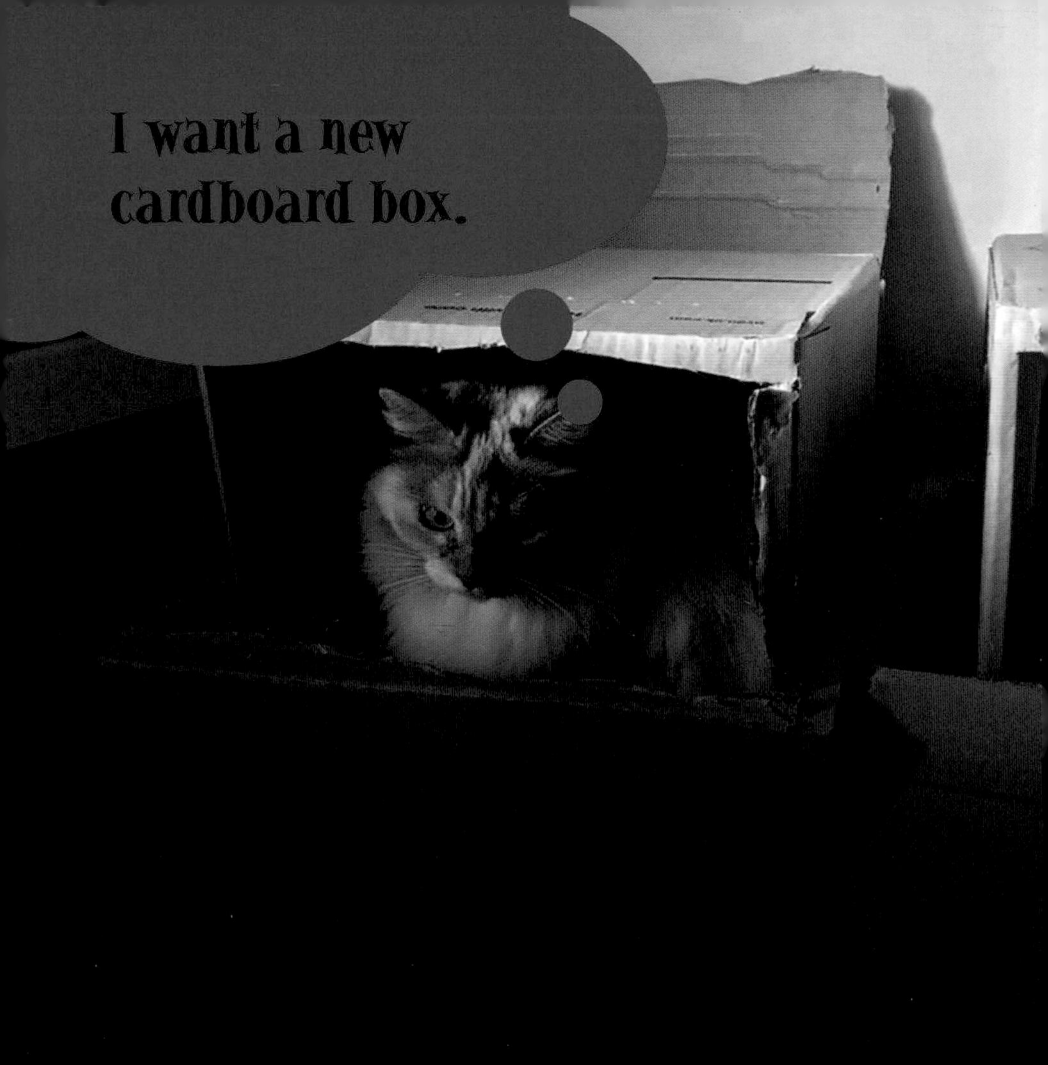
I want a new cardboard box.

The cat flap is closed again. I can't go eat next door's cat's food.

I don't know what to do next. I finished messing up the house ages ago.

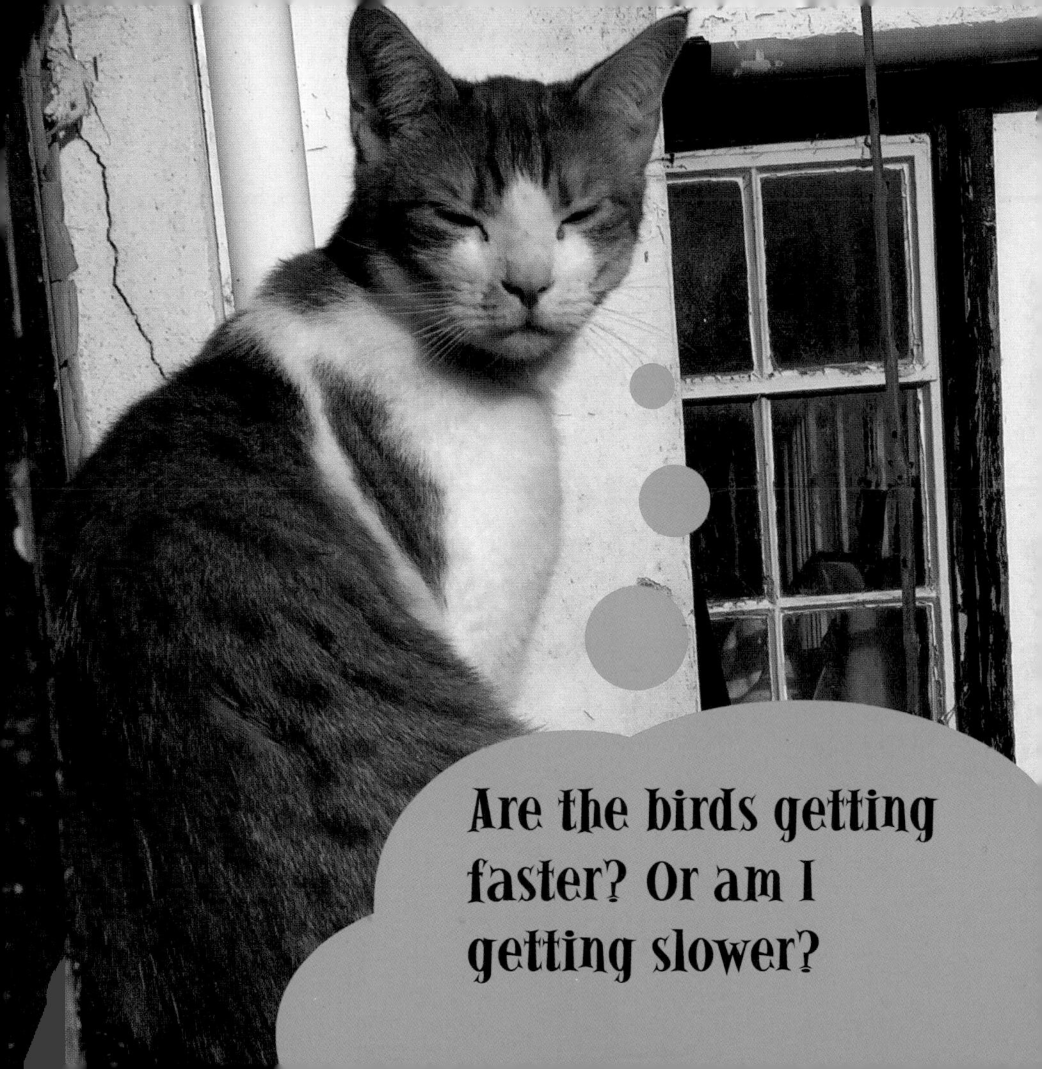
Are the birds getting faster? Or am I getting slower?

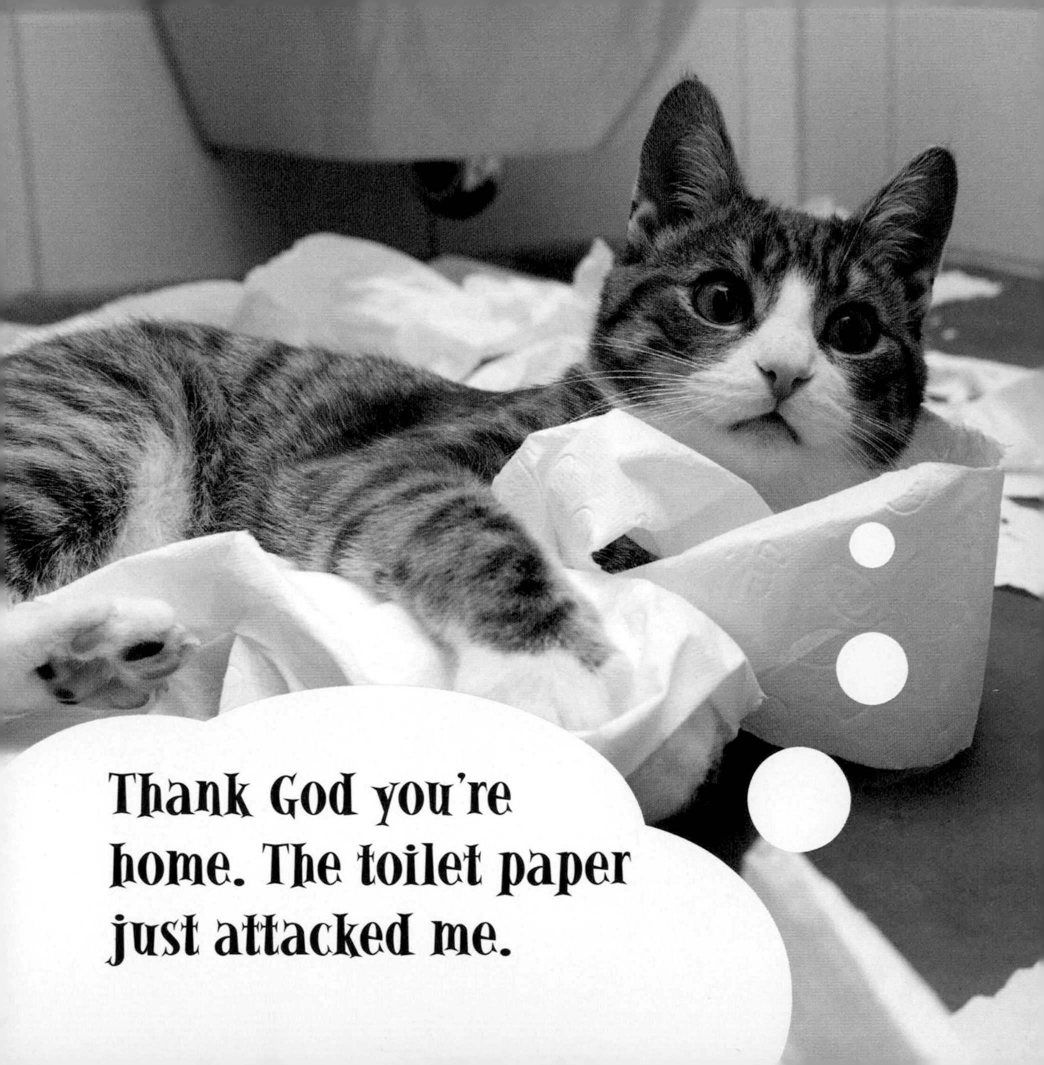
Thank God you're home. The toilet paper just attacked me.

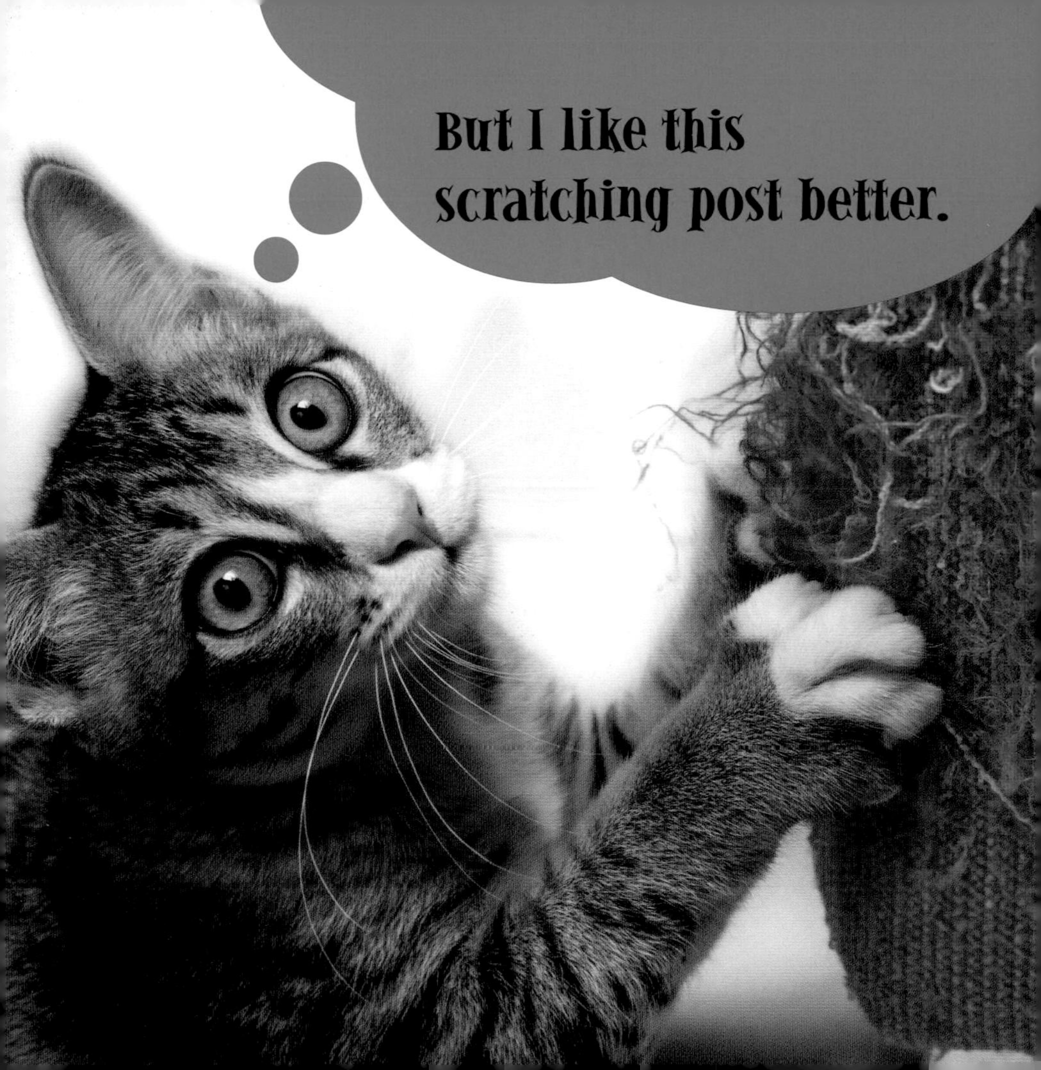
But I like this scratching post better.

I don't want anything. But I keep meowing and my owner still hasn't woken up.

She stopped rubbing
my tummy just before
I could attack her.

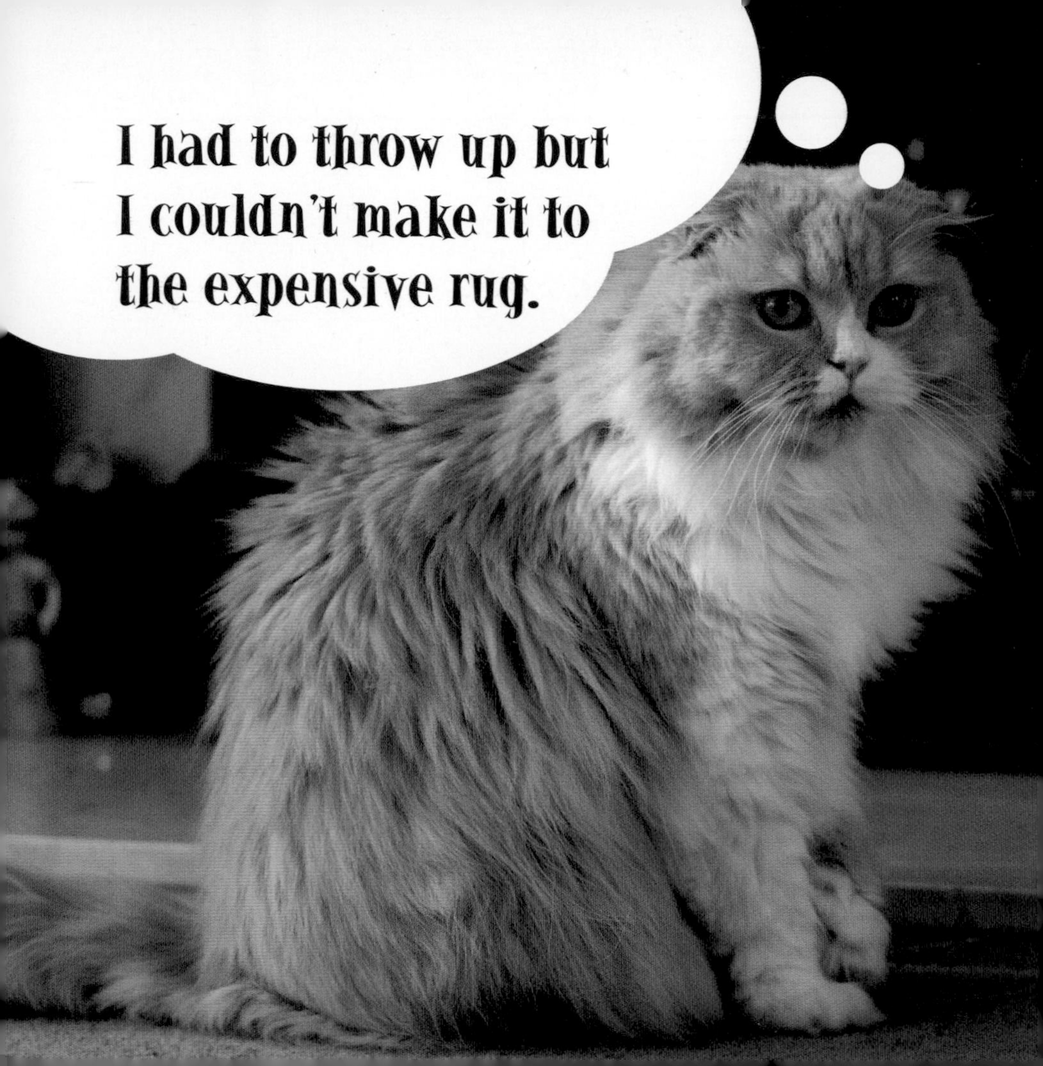
I had to throw up but I couldn't make it to the expensive rug.

I destroyed the sofa, but no one has noticed yet.

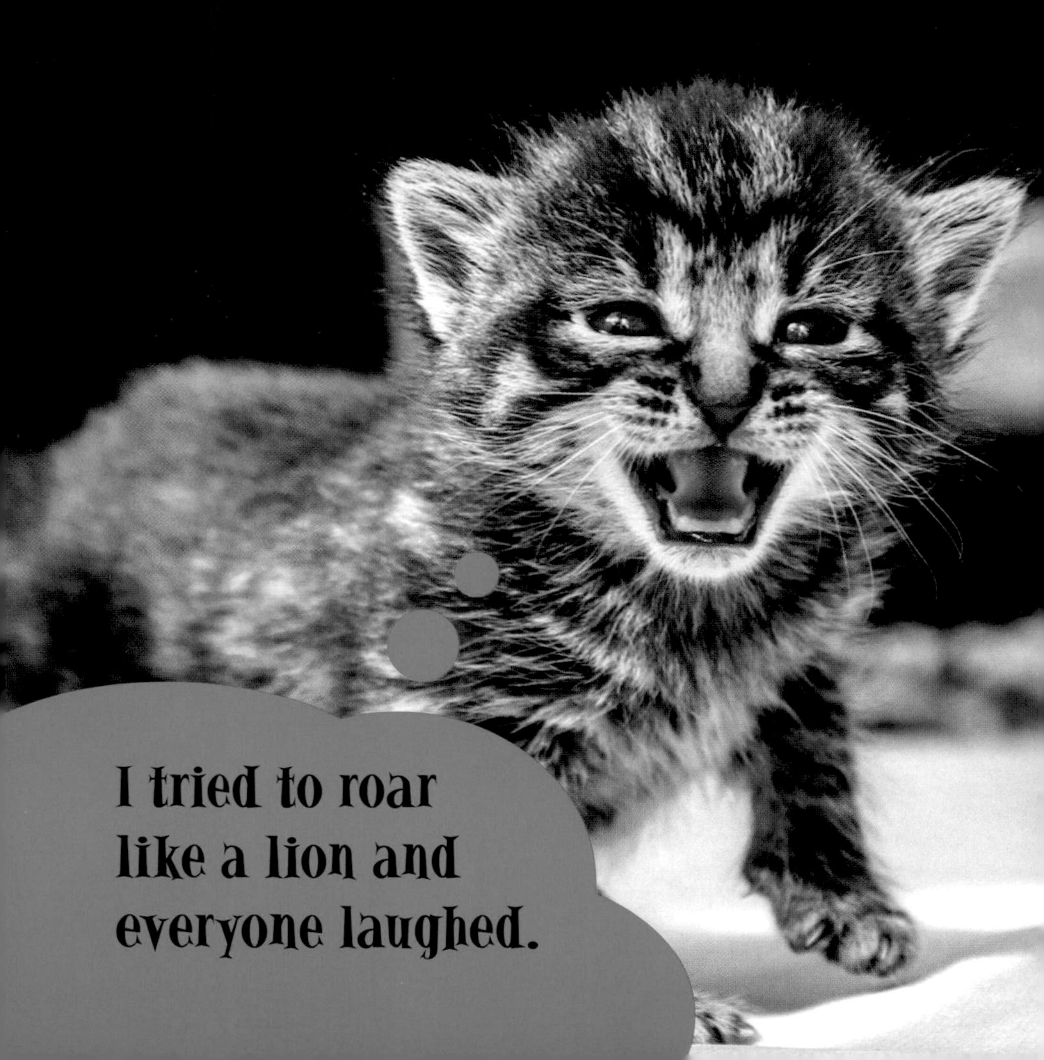
I tried to roar like a lion and everyone laughed.

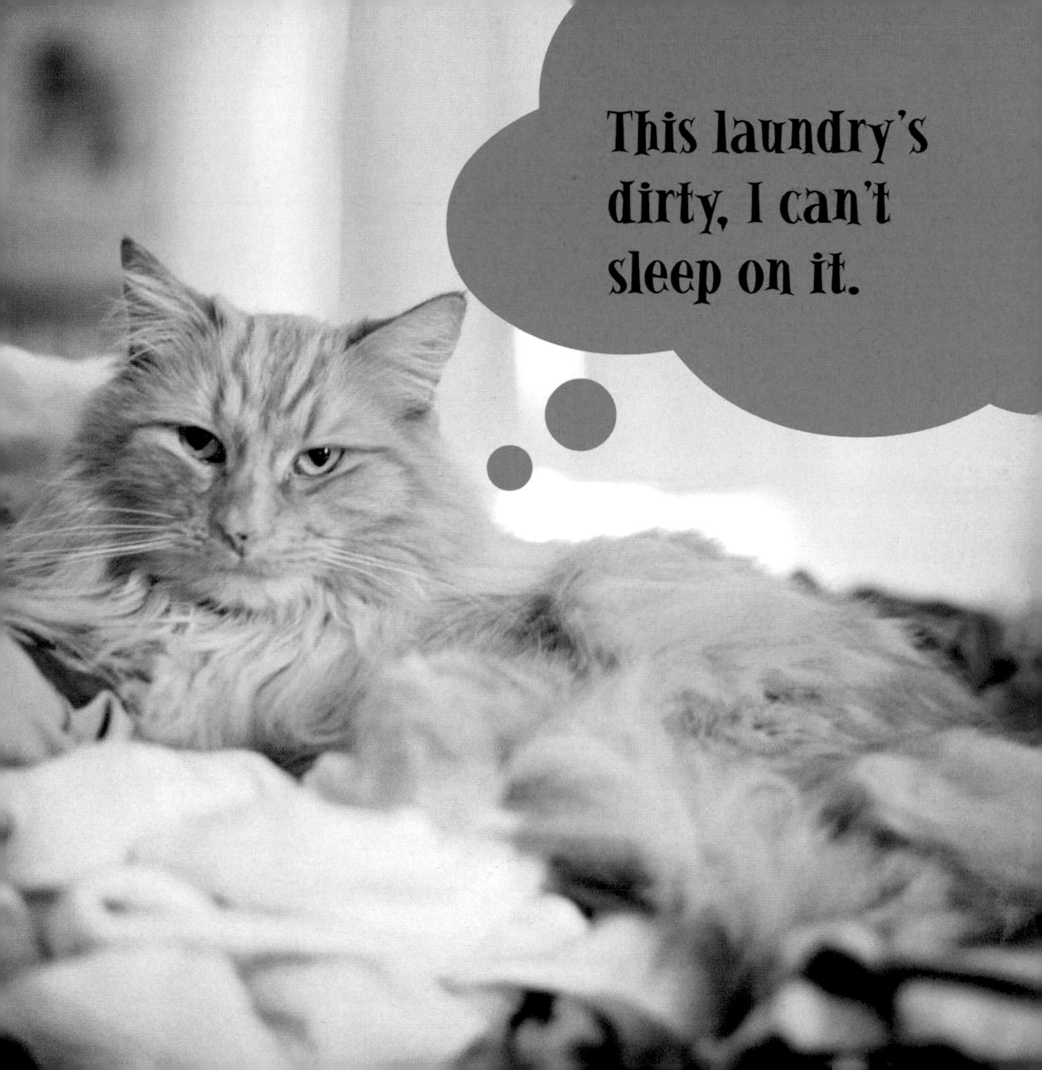
This laundry's dirty, I can't sleep on it.

My owner doesn't like
the headless bird I gave her.

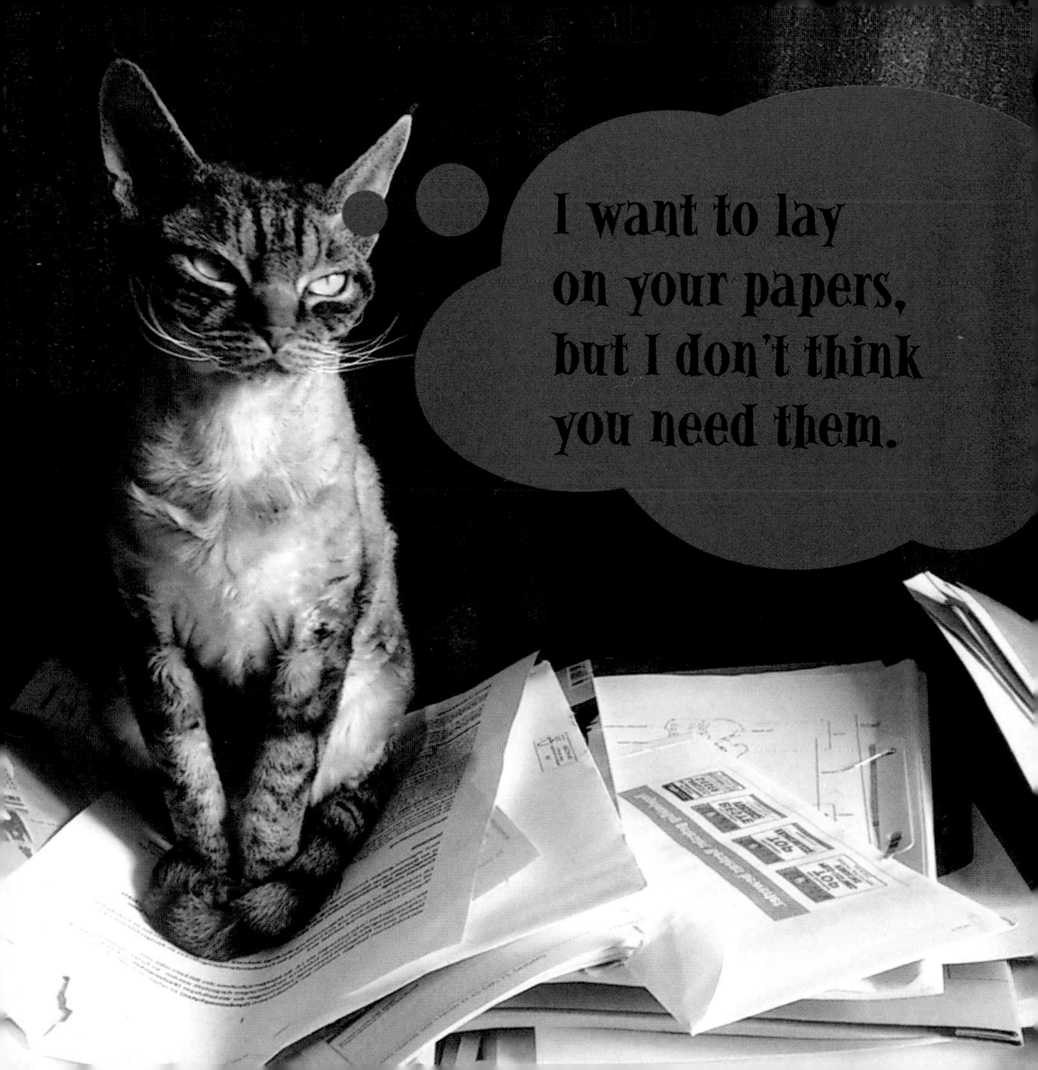
I want to lay on your papers, but I don't think you need them.

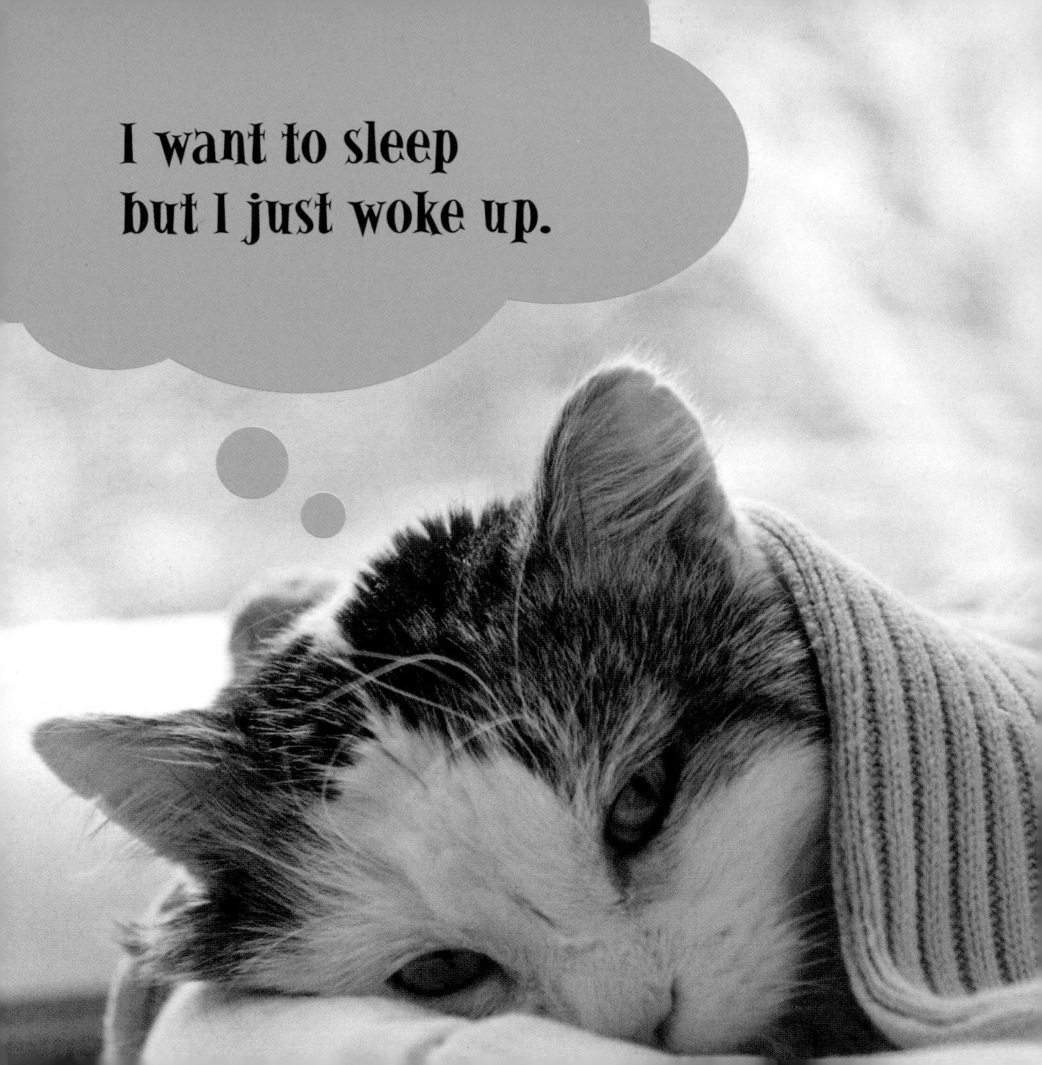
I want to sleep
but I just woke up.

It's really nice outside but it's also really nice inside.

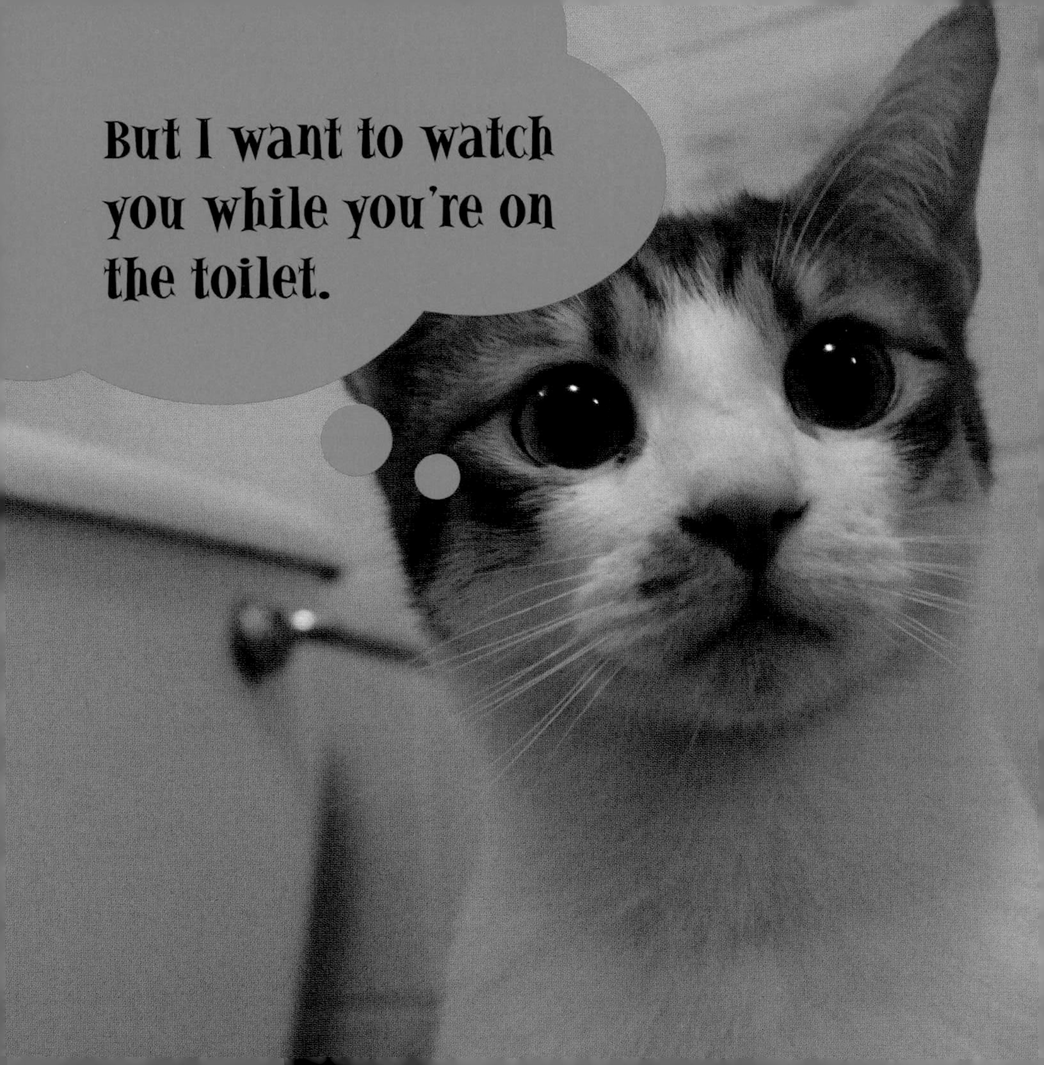
But I want to watch you while you're on the toilet.

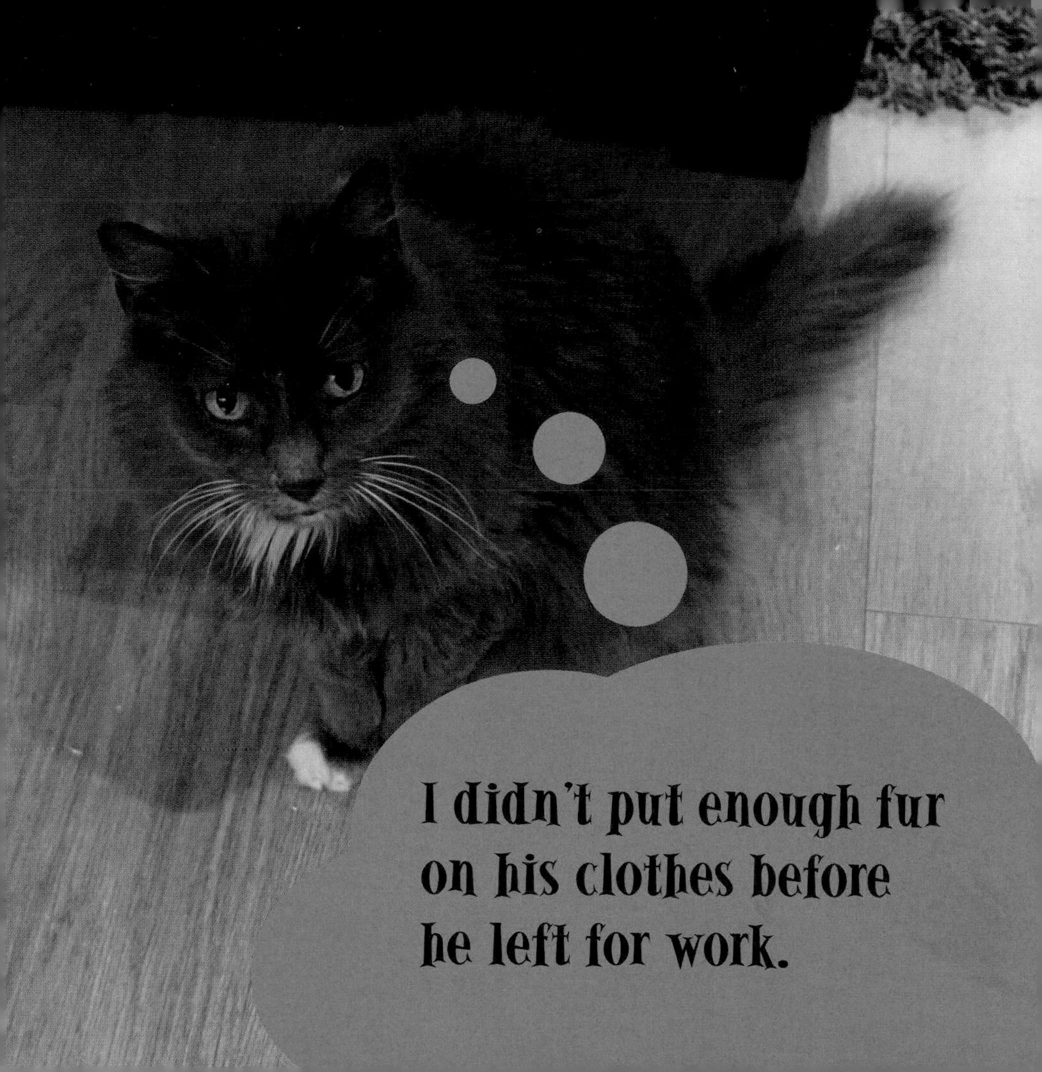
I didn't put enough fur
on his clothes before
he left for work.

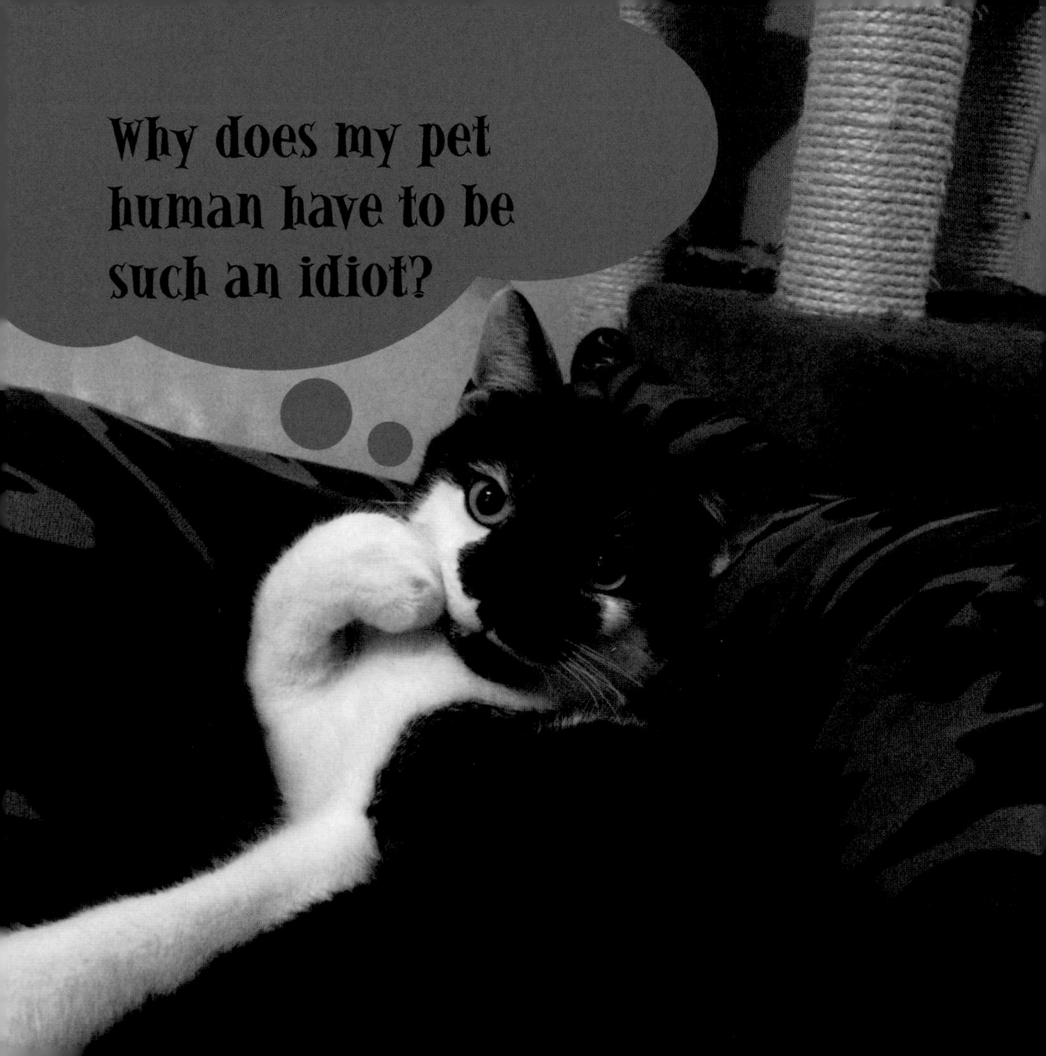
Why does my pet human have to be such an idiot?

Do I chase the red dot because it exists? Or does it exist because I chase it?

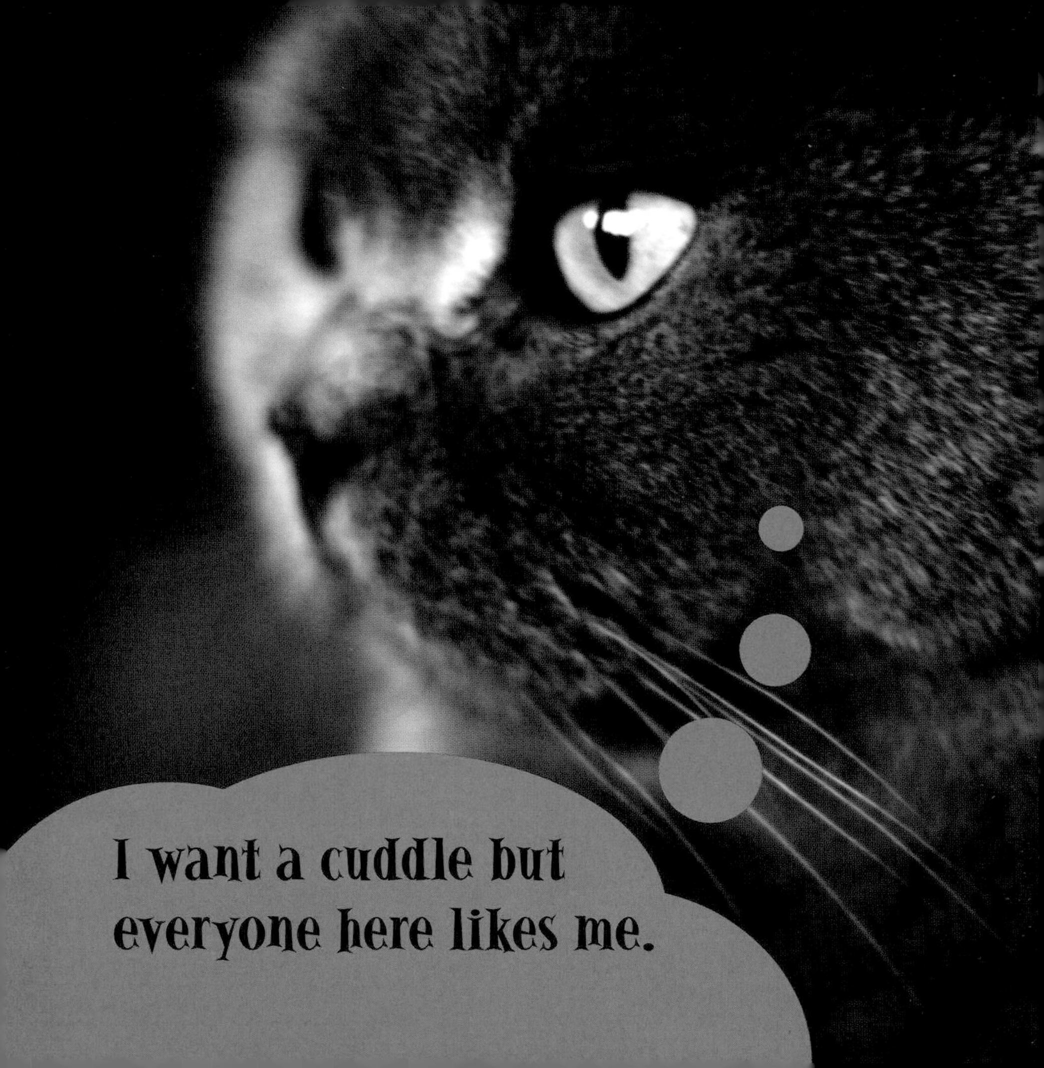
I want a cuddle but
everyone here likes me.

I'm running out of storage space under the sofa for all my toys.

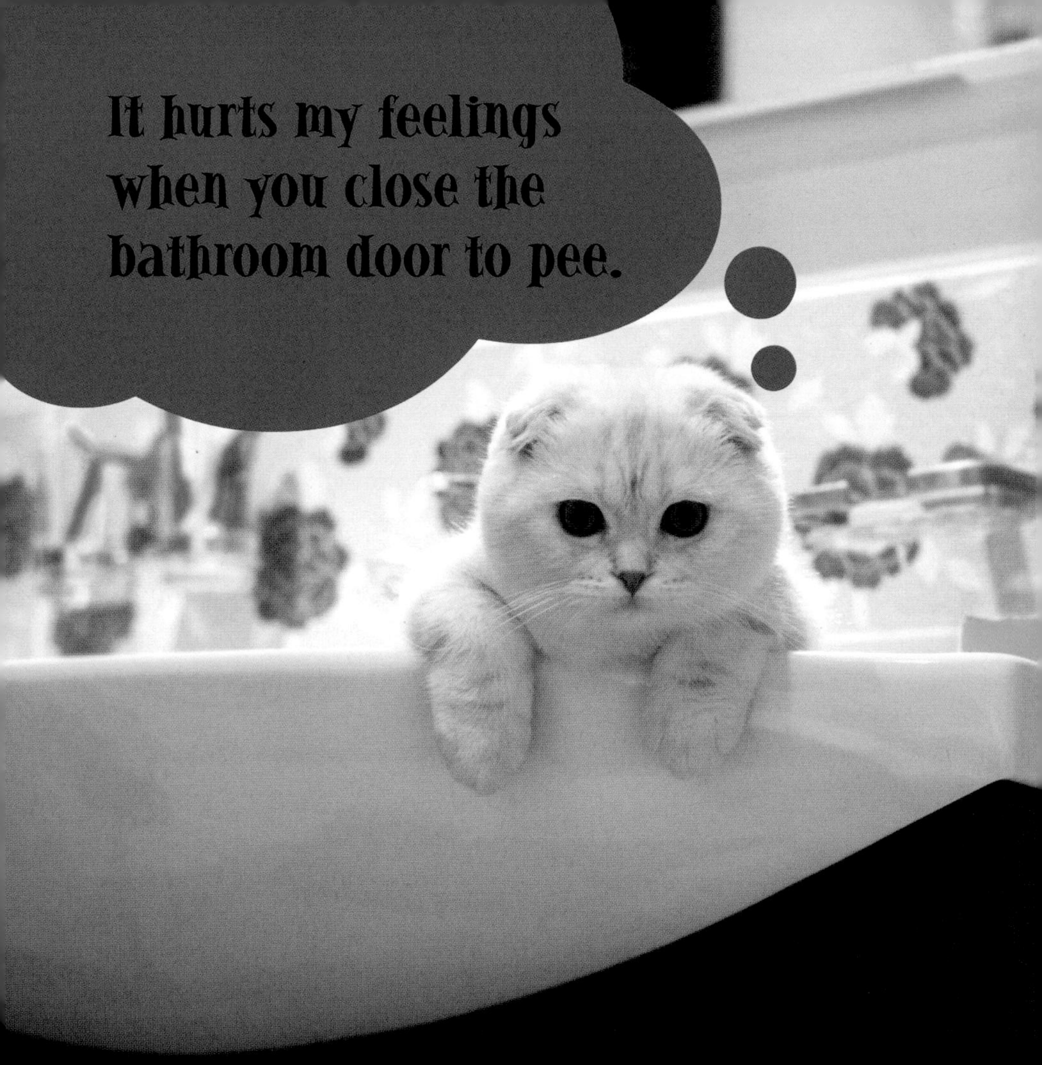
It hurts my feelings when you close the bathroom door to pee.

My owner vacuumed today and now I'm missing a rubber band, some pieces of string and my favourite bottle cap.

If this laptop's not for sitting on, then why is it so warm?

But I wanted the diamanté collar...

I just don't understand why YOU can't sleep on the floor tonight.

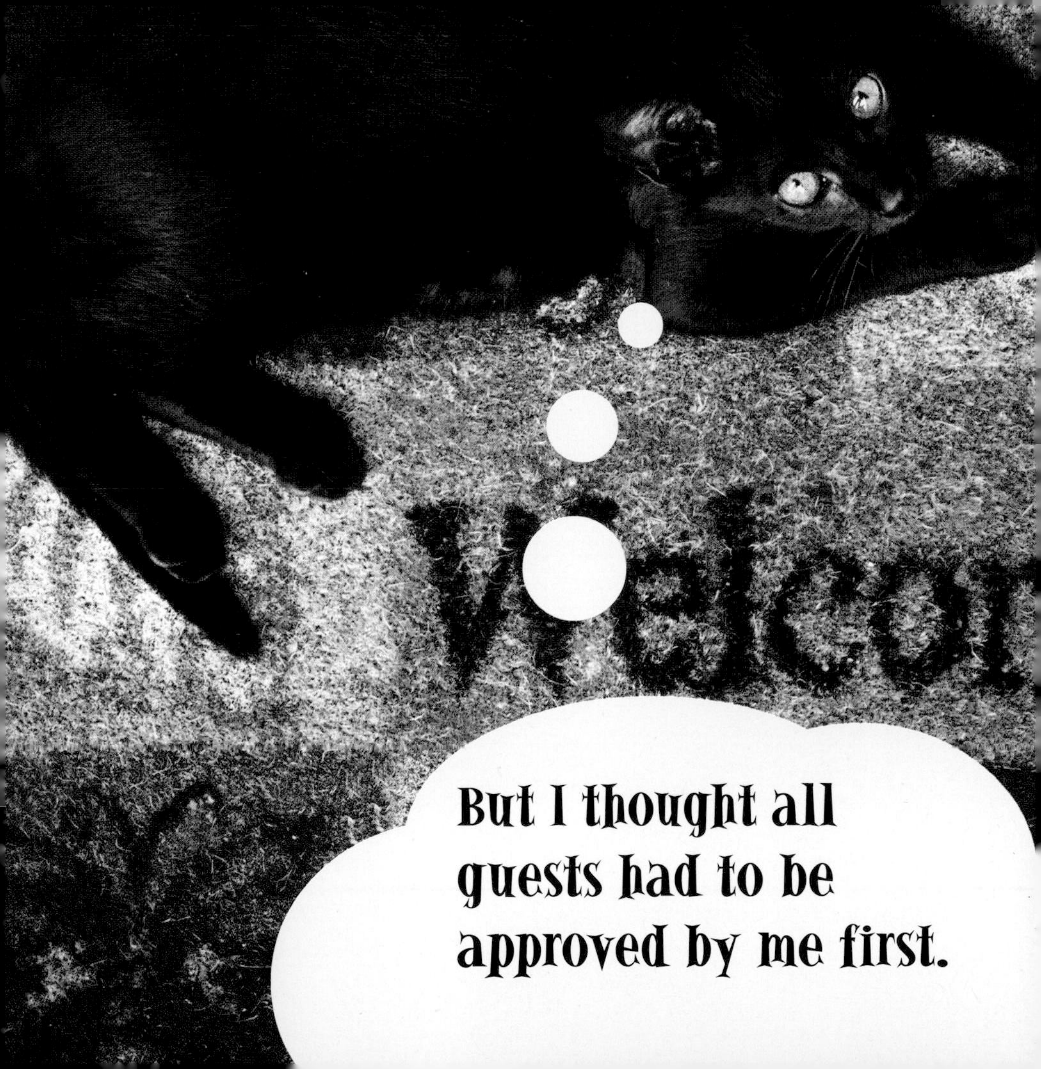
But I thought all guests had to be approved by me first.

Next door's cat's food is from Waitrose.

I spend more time looking for a toy to play with than actually playing with one.

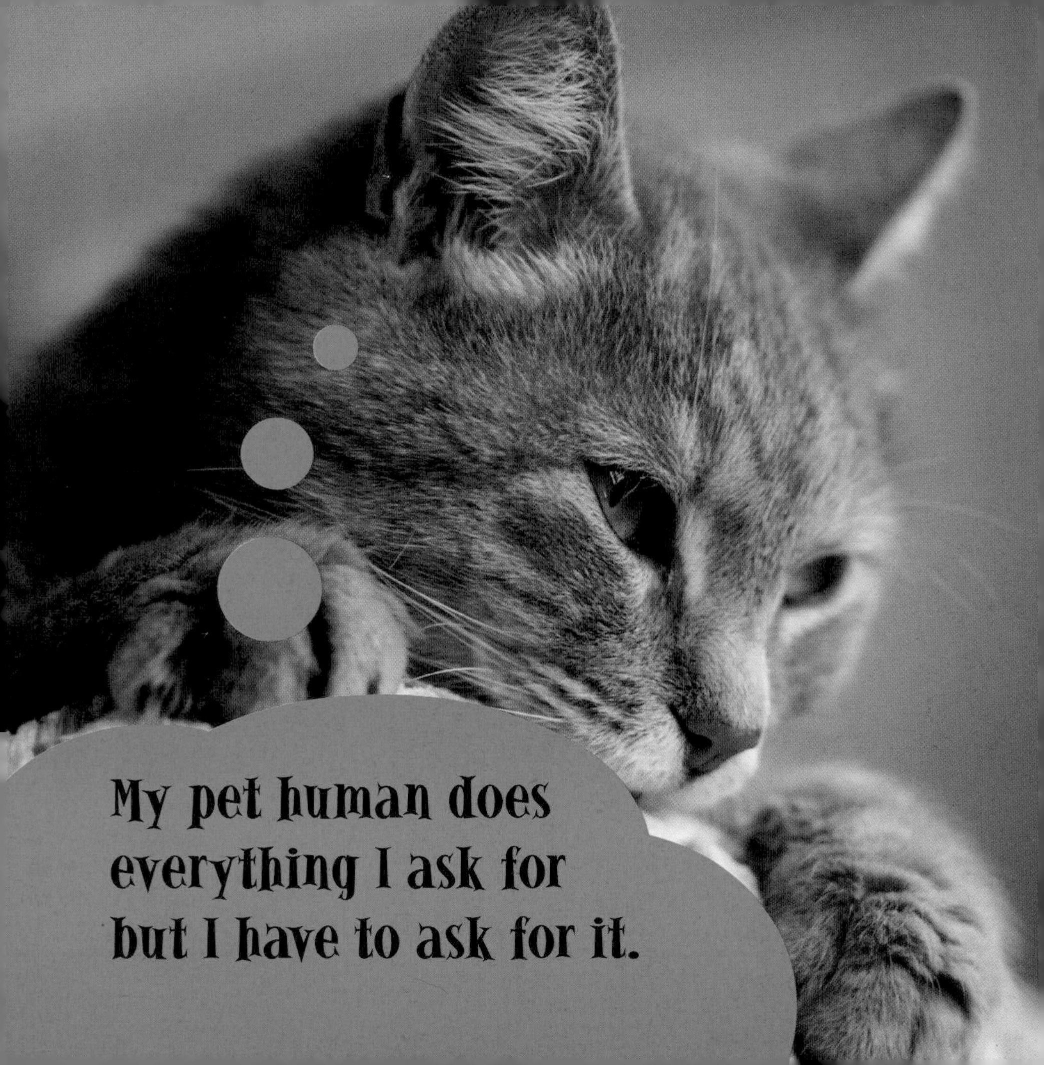
My pet human does
everything I ask for
but I have to ask for it.

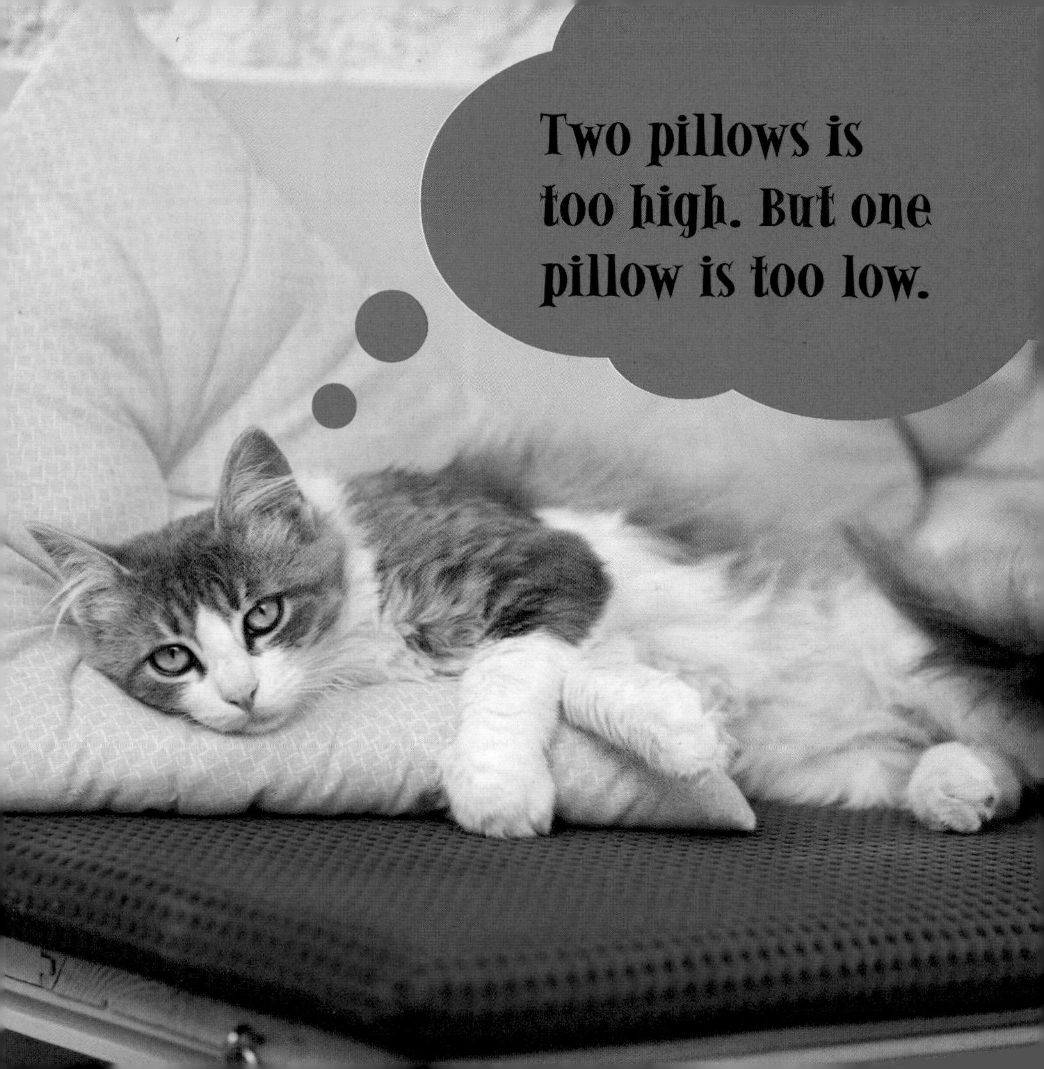
Two pillows is too high. But one pillow is too low.

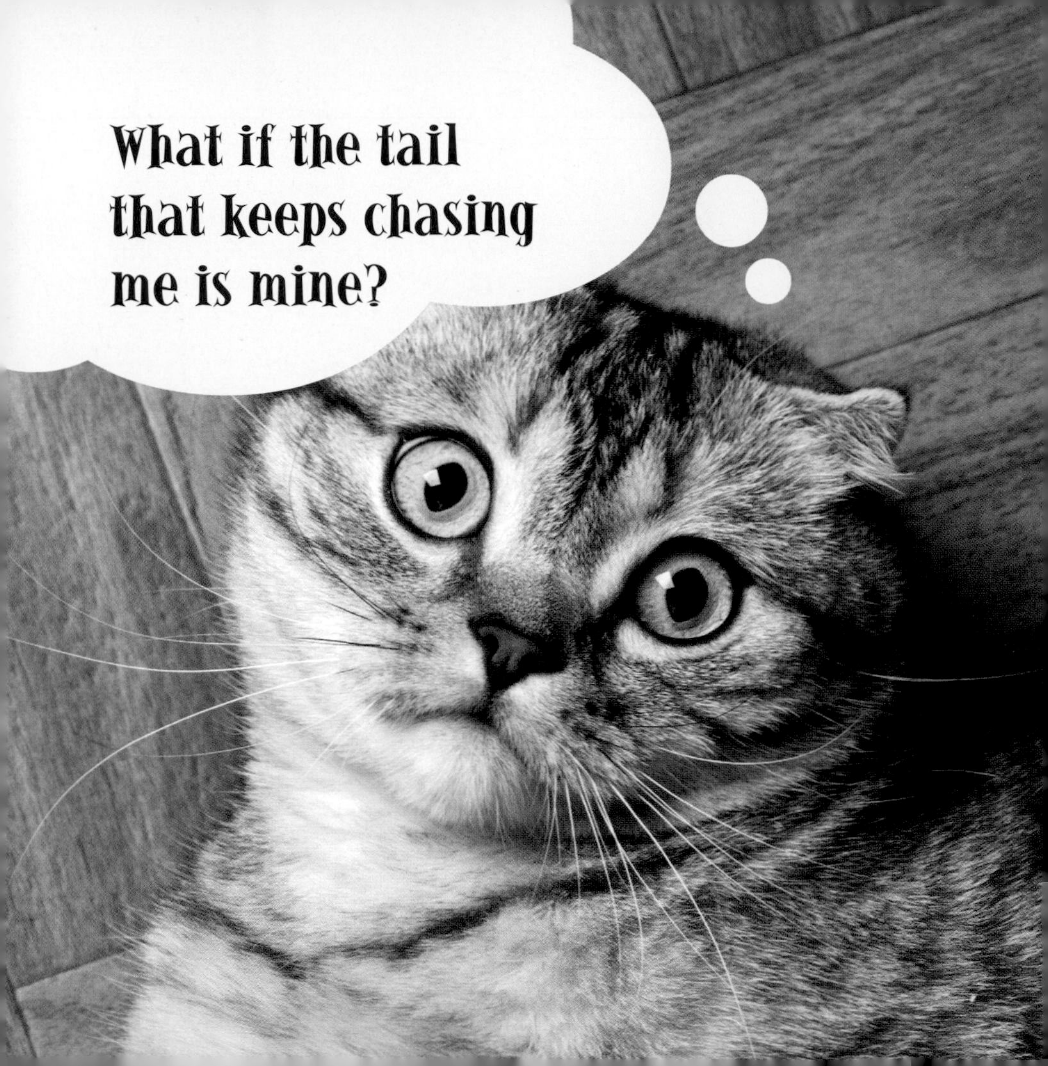
What if the tail
that keeps chasing
me is mine?

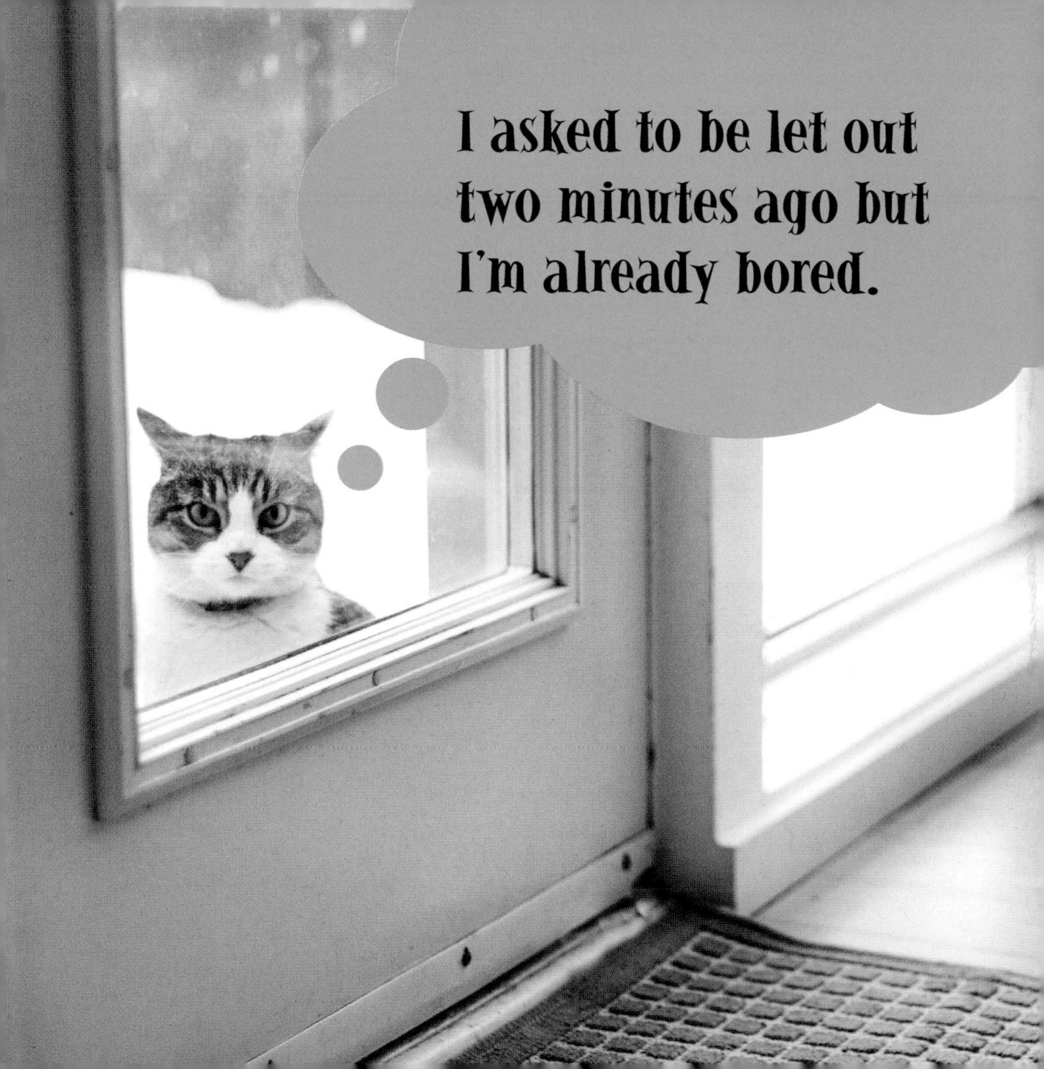
I asked to be let out two minutes ago but I'm already bored.

I can't believe next door's cat gave me fleas. I thought we were friends.

When I finally caught the feather toy, I realised there was no point.

My owner put my favourite blanket in the wash.

I really want to catch that fly but this bed is too comfortable.

I lick my owner but she never licks me back.

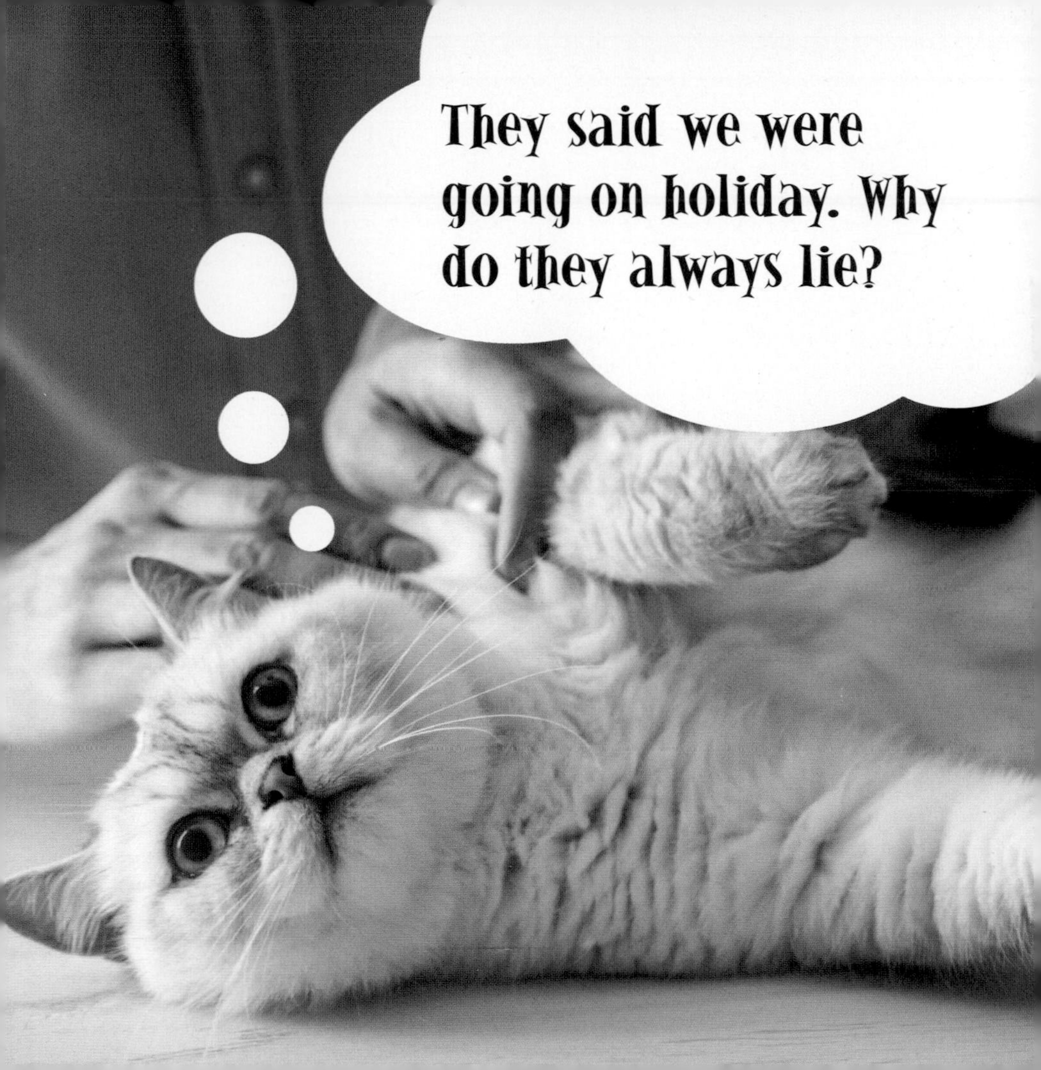
They said we were going on holiday. Why do they always lie?

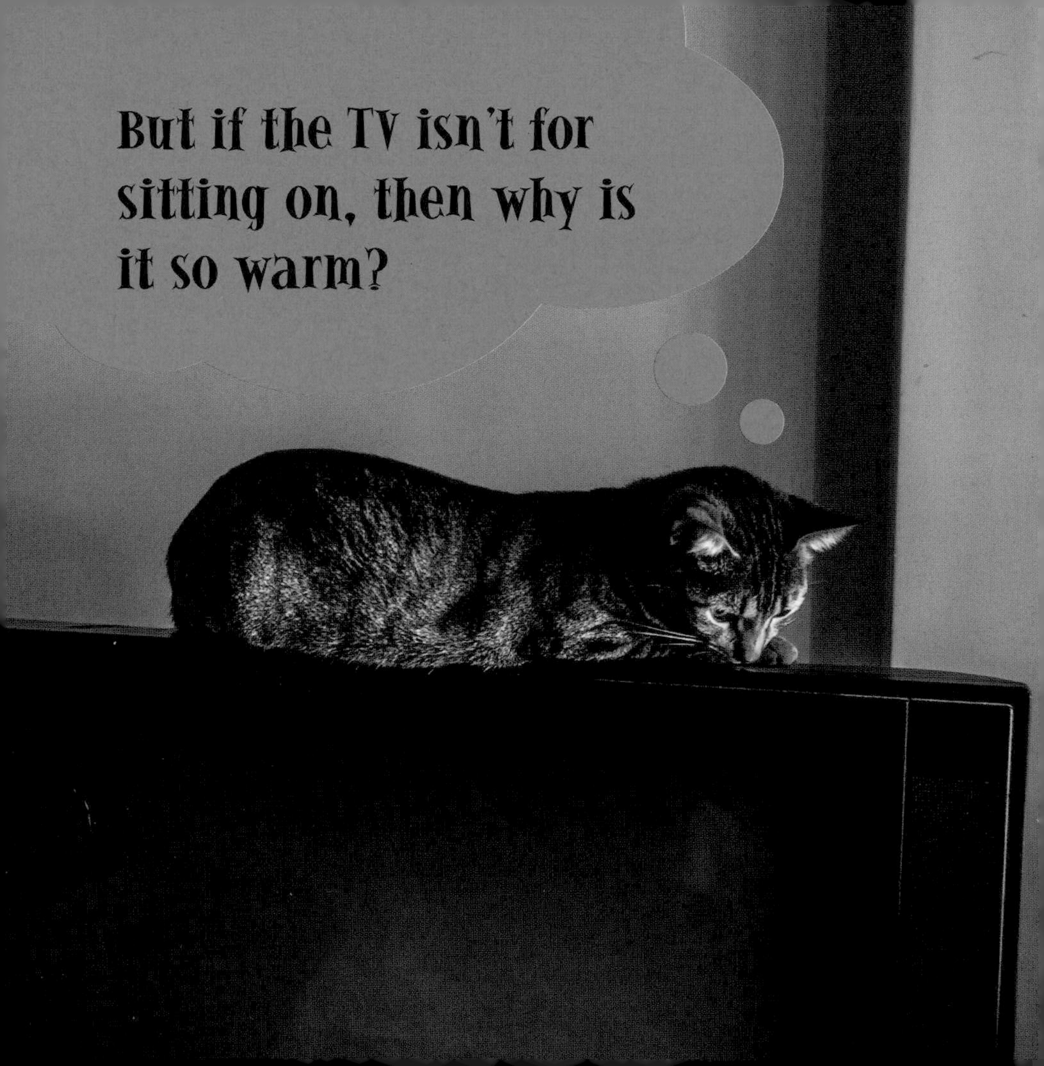
But if the TV isn't for sitting on, then why is it so warm?

What is my life and how did I get here?

I did a poop on the carpet, but my owner didn't step on it.

I just wanted to 'inspect' their dinner.

Photo credits

1 iStock
2 iStock
3 iStock
4 iStock
5 iStock
6 iStock
7 iStock
8 iStock
9 iStock
10 iStock
11 iStock
12 Oleg Kozlov / Alamy Stock Photo
13 iStock
14 iStock
15 iStock
16 iStock
17 iStock
18 Karen Finn
19 iStock
20 Karen Finn
21 Doris Rudd/ GettyImages
22 iStock
23 iStock
24 iStock
25 iStock
26 iStock
27 Victoria Wort
28 iStock
29 iStock
30 Lola Wolsey
31 iStock
32 iStock
33 iStock
34 iStock
35 iStock
36 Sarah Garnham
37 iStock
38 iStock
39 Steph Naulls
40 Anna Mrowiec
41 iStock
42 iStock
43 iStock
44 Karen Plum
45 iStock
46 iStock
47 iStock
48 Gonalo Barriga/ GettyImages
49 Anna Mrowiec
50 iStock
51 iStock
52 iStock
53 iStock
54 iStock
55 Shutterstock
56 Steph Naulls
57 iStock
58 Charlotte Warner
59 iStock
60 Emily Yau
61 iStock
62 iStock
63 iStock
64 iStock
65 iStock
66 iStock
67 iStock
68 iStock
69 Lauren Quinn
70 Leah Feltham
71 iStock
72 iStock
73 iStock
74 iStock
75 iStock
76 iStock
77 iStock
78 Benjamin McConnell
79 iStock
80 iStock
81 iStock
82 Karen Finn
83 iStock
84 iStock
85 Charlotte Warner
86 iStock
87 iStock
88 iStock
89 iStock
90 iStock
91 iStock
92 iStock
93 iStock
94 iStock
95 Alexandra Böcker/EyeEm/ GettyImages
96 iStock
97 iStock
98 Charlotte Warner
99 Benjamin McConnell
100 Rowan Thornber
101 Karen Plum
102 Sam Morgan
103 iStock
104 iStock
105 iStock
106 iStock
107 iStock
108 iStock
109 iStock
110 iStock
111 iStock
112 iStock
113 iStock
114 iStock
115 iStock
116 iStock
117 iStock
118 iStock
119 iStock
120 Emily Yau
121 iStock
122 José Eduardo Nucci/ GettyImages
123 iStock
124 Emily Yau
125 Anna Mrowiec